# Sarum Chronicle

## Recent historical research on Salisbury & district

### Issue 17: 2017

ISBN 978-0-9571692-8-9       ISSN: 1475-1844

How to contact us:
   To order a copy phone Ruth Newman on 01722 328922 or email ruth.tanglewood@btinternet.com
   For other titles in the *Sarum Studies* series and for back issues of *Sarum Chronicle* please contact Jane Howells on 01722 331426 or email as below.
   To submit material for consideration in future editions of *Sarum Chronicle* email Jane Howells at jane@sarum-editorial.co.uk with the words Sarum Chronicle in the subject line.

Editorial Team: Roy Bexon, John Chandler, John Cox, John Elliott, Jane Howells, Andrew Minting, Ruth Newman, Margaret Smith.

Practical and editorial assistance from Chris Clark, Kate Crouch, Penelope Rundle and Peter Saunders.

www.sarumchronicle.wordpress.com

Designed and typeset by John Chandler

# Contents

# Editorial

Now in its 17th year, *Sarum Chronicle* is the successor to the *Hatcher Review*, a biannual local history periodical which ran for 25 years and 50 issues until 2000. That was the brainchild of the redoubtable Lady Paskin of Great Wishford (or Wishford Magna, as she always gave her address), deaf but determined and very old, and one of a cavalcade of colourful Salisbury historians who have enriched my intellectual life. She published my first paper in issue 5, not long after the start of the *Hatcher Review* in 1976. That year of the long hot summer (and my first in Salisbury), 1976, was when – coincidentally – a letter appeared in the *Salisbury Journal* proposing the formation of a local history group, to be based at the newly-established Arts Centre in the former St Edmund's Church. The group was set up the following year, and two days ago (as I write, in May 2017) I was invited to join in their 40th anniversary celebration, with cake and fruit juice (nothing stronger as we were meeting in the Salvation Army hall).

Almost uniquely, I should think, Salisbury Local History Group has always held weekly lectures or outings, on Tuesdays, through much of each year, a kind of slow but steady beating heart consistently pumping local history through the city. Very many of those lecturers and their subjects have subsequently found their way into the pages of the *Hatcher Review* or the *Sarum Chronicle*, and all five of us who started the latter were there, with about 70 others of the group, to enjoy the cake. There were many absences too, of course, because none of us go on forever.

Much of the enjoyment of such occasions derives from being reminded of old affectionate friendships, and swapping anecdotes about their eccentricities. Four names in particular kept cropping up: Bill Garrett, first chairman, and Audrey Martingell, first secretary, whose deaths within a few weeks of each other in 1995 inflicted a cruel blow on the group. Jim Smith, one of the group's speakers, and (with his wife Mary) a long-term member, who wrote and illustrated children's books from his 'Little Junk Shop' beside the Greencroft. And then there was Michael Charlton, life and soul of the group almost from its inception until his death, as president, in 2008. Mike was a professional artist – like Jim a children's book illustrator – who in later life turned his attention to one of his other loves, local history subjects, and his work graces this issue's cover. There were others in this cavalcade, too, including one very much alive, whose 90th birthday that day we also celebrated.

We – the group and the *Chronicle* – are part of a continuum. The group enthuses people to learn about the history of their surroundings. They then learn how to research that history for themselves, to present talks about what they have discovered, and go on to write it all up to be published (more than 1,000 pages of it in the *Chronicle* since we started, and the tally growing year by year). Then it is there in print for others to enjoy in perpetuity, to become enthusiastic about, and to use in their own researches in turn. And so on.

So we hope that you will find the present offering as interesting, varied and stimulating as its predecessors. It benefits enormously, I should add, from the sterling work of Roy Bexon in preparing the images that accompany the text. We also hope that, 40 years from now, when the group celebrates its 80th birthday and the *Chronicle* its 57th issue, our successors will look back with gratitude and affection – and still find something in these pages worth reading.

*John Chandler*

# Glimpses into the Intriguing History of the Former Art Shop at 102 Crane Street

## Louise Purdy

For many years 102 Crane Street in Salisbury was known as 'The Compleat Artist', a specialist art supplies shop run by Martyn Kennard since 1980. Those who knew this popular art shop or at least this area of Salisbury will remember the various bright colour schemes Martyn applied to it. Sadly, he died in 2013 and the art shop has since been closed. Although unlisted, this building is in close proximity to the historic Crane Bridge and a number of other grade I and II listed buildings in Crane Street.

Fig 1 – The former art shop at 102 Crane Street, Salisbury with the Freemasons Hall to the east side (May 2016)

102 Crane Street, a rather unusual but quaint assortment of small single storey buildings merged together is dwarfed by its neighbour the imposing Freemasons Hall, but it does in fact have a longer history (Fig 1).

In early 2016, the Wiltshire Buildings Record (WBR) was instructed to prepare a heritage statement on 102 Crane Street.[1] This article is primarily based on what was discovered about its history by the WBR, but also refers to the recollections of Miss Edna Trott, a previous tenant who ran the art shop from 1954 to 1970. Her recollections were recorded in a newsletter of the former Salisbury & District Preservation Trust in 1982. The Trust later evolved into the Salisbury Civic Society.[2]

In May 2016, Dorothy Treasure, Principal Buildings Historian at the WBR recorded and interpreted the building at 102 Crane Street and I conducted documentary research into its history. The former art shop, by this point had been cleared of its contents giving Dorothy good access to the physical fabric of the building.

Fig 2 - North-east and north-west elevations of 102 Crane Street (May 2016)

Much of interest was discovered just looking at the exterior of the building. The north-east and north-west elevations closest to the River Avon were of particular interest for a number of reasons (Fig 2).

Firstly, they show the extent of the building under which a culverted section of the River Avon flows. It is not apparent to most passers-by that a tributary of the River Avon is flowing directly below the former shop and under part of the riverside pavement on which they are walking. A grille can be found along part of the north-east elevation of the building exposing the river water below.

Secondly, the north-east and north-west elevations show what appears to be a mid-19th century gabled and part slate-tiled bridge across the culverted section of the River Avon. It is incorporated into the building with entry through a reused and remodelled 17th century boarded door set into a mid-19th century Tudor-arched moulded doorway. The gable contains a king-post with ogee raking struts. The wall-plates project slightly beyond the face and once supported barge-boards.

Thirdly, next to the doorway is a blank area of wall, an infill, possibly of rendered concrete block with a shallow-pitched lean-to roof against the main double-pitched roof, both covered in Welsh slate. To the right is a flat-roofed formerly projecting bay window infilled with blocks of cut stone flush with the exterior. The window was subsequently cut through, possibly in the period 1887 to 1900, for a doorway. Above is a moulded crenellated stone parapet. To the right of the bay is a blank rendered wall, the extension added in the late 19th century.

Historical research suggests that this part of 102 Crane Street originally had a dual role as both a summer house and a bridge to an island in the River Avon close to Crane Bridge. Many older inhabitants of Salisbury may remember this island as late as the early 1980s. Salisbury City Council then restructured this section of the River Avon, resulting in the widening of the river, the loss of the island and the development of the riverside walk.

The oldest part of the present building first appears on an 1854 plan of the sewerage and drainage scheme in Salisbury, straddling the river to the west of a detached residence called Retreat Cottage. This cottage, since demolished faced onto Crane Street with a garden and walkways in front (Fig 3).[3]

On the west side can be seen the outlines of the open porch to the bridge walk and south of this, the projecting square bay window. On the east side are two small lean-to buildings, which later maps indicate were gone by 1901. The building was decorated in Gothick style with pitched roofs decorated with bargeboards at the gables.

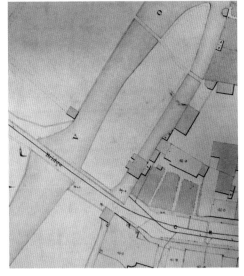

Fig 3 - Extract from the Local Board of Health plan of the City's sewerage and drainage scheme in 1854 showing part of the building now known as 102 Crane Street and the island in the River Avon to the east.

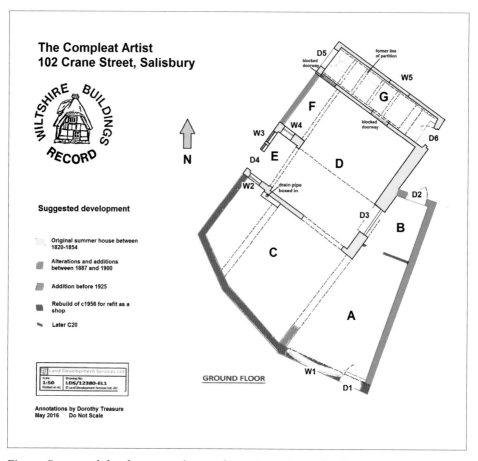

The Compleat Artist
102 Crane Street, Salisbury

WILTSHIRE BUILDINGS RECORD

N

**Suggested development**

Original summer house between 1820-1854

Alterations and additions between 1887 and 1900

Addition before 1925

Rebuild of c1956 for refit as a shop

Later C20

Land Development Services Ltd

| Scale | Drawing No: |
| 1:50 | LDS/12380-EL1 |
| Plotted on A1 | © Land Development Services Ltd. 20? |

Annotations by Dorothy Treasure
May 2016    Do Not Scale

D5
blocked doorway

former line of partition

W5

F

G

W3    W4

D4    E

D

blocked doorway

D6

W2    drain pipe boxed in

D2

D3

B

C

A

GROUND FLOOR

W1

D1

Fig 4 – Suggested development phases of 102 Crane Street by the WBR (May 2016).

This original building was interpreted by the WBR as being a picturesque Gothick summer house and it is very likely it belonged to a neighbouring property, Retreat Cottage at this stage. Its purpose was probably twofold; a summer house that perhaps also acted as an artist's studio. In 1861, it is known an artist occupied Retreat Cottage.[4]

An easel set up in the north–west bay window would have given good light in the afternoon for painting. This was accessed separately on the east side from the gardens of Retreat Cottage. A separate covered bridge incorporated on the north side gave access to the island, with an internal door in the centre into the unheated summer house.  If the summer house was occupied by an artist for a time, this may explain some of its creative features.

An annotated plan of the site was produced by the WBR showing their best interpretation of the development phases of sections of the building (Fig 4).

The WBR believes that the summer house may have a construction date between 1820 and 1854 as the features of the original building suggest this and there is no evidence yet of this building featuring on any map dated any earlier than the mid-19th century. Suggested development phases take into account the changing footprint shown by Ordnance Survey (OS) maps from the late-19th to the mid-20th century (Fig 5).[5]

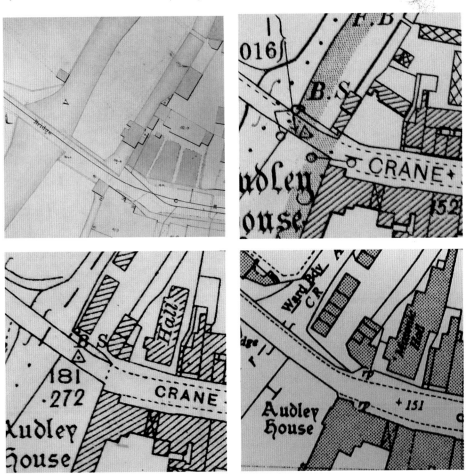

Fig 5 - Extract from the 1854 map (top left) compared to extracts from OS maps published in 1901 (top right), 1925 (bottom left) and 1953 (bottom right)

Looking closer at the bridge (area G), the doorway (D5) leading from the river path is now blocked by a WC. It is likely the door was originally positioned further back along the bridge and there was an open porch in front of it. (Figs 4, 6). This 17th century boarded door is hung on decoratively-moulded strap hinges with expanded ends. The head of the door is 4-centred, and a moulded frame with fillets covering the gaps between the boards applied on the face. A drop-loop handle from a decoratively-cut back plate is still extant (Figs 6, 7).[6]

Fig 6 (left) External view of boarded door and surround. (May 2016).
Fig 7 (right) The drop-loop handle with a decoratively-cut back plate. (May 2016).
Fig 8 (above) Bay E showing three windows (W2-4) and blocked door (D4) (May 2016)

A further blocked door is found next to the W.C. facing south-west. The site of a second external door leading onto the island before the extension into area F was constructed.

The north-east wall, forming part of the bridge contains a blocked transomed and mullioned window (W5) with diagonally-set retaining bars and decorative turnbuckle catches. From the outside this blocked window is visible surrounded by a geometric design (Fig 2).

Turning to the north-west wall of the original summer house beyond the gable end; it is divided into two bays. Area E was a bay window that looked out onto the island. Area F was an extension that was formed at some time between 1887 and 1900, possibly when the shed, area C was built onto the front (Figs 4, 5).

Bay E appears to be made up of a three-sided hollow and roll-moulded mullioned bay with three separate windows, possibly reused on this site. These are set on top of what appears to be ashlar work, flush with the exterior edge of the windows. The inside of the wall below the fenestration was, and still is partly lined with vertical boarding. To the left of the forward-facing light, a narrow boarded door (D4) has been cut through, possibly between 1887 and 1900, very probably along with other changes, including the blocking up of the rest of the forward-facing window. D4 is hung on cast iron hinges and has a rim lock (Figs 4, 8).

The ceiling above the former bay window is extraordinary, containing what appears to be fine plasterwork giving the impression of flat fan-vaulting. The ribs form long mouchettes in semi-circles at the centre and pairs of quarter circles at each end, with shorter ones between. The ribs spring from moulded bosses, one of which incorporates a gilded bunch of grapes. On either side of the semi-circular fan-vault are narrow panels containing blank shields flanked by flat scrolls. The cavetto cornice is also studded with decorative bosses (Figs 9-13).

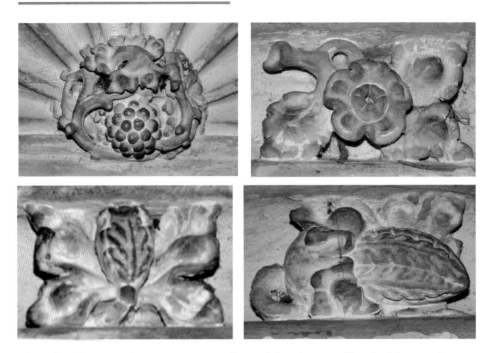

Figs 9 (previous page), 10, 11, 12, 13  - Part of the plaster ceiling looking north-east, a boss at the centre of a fan-vault and examples of acanthus and fleuron devices and a stylised bud on the cornice. (May 2016)

The WBR conclusion is that the fine quality of the plasterwork, some of which retains good quality gilding and carpentry, is contemporary with the early to mid-19th century build. The remainder of the ceiling in the original building is plain and barrel vaulted and formed over horizontal boarding.

The origins of the 17th century door, the moulded stone parapet over the original square bay, the stone window frame and the fine plaster ceiling in the bay remain a mystery. All that the WBR can conclude it is likely that some of these pieces came from elsewhere and were reused, whilst other features were purpose-made at some cost during the building's construction in the early to mid-19th century.

Miss Edna Trott recollected, as reported in the newsletter of the Salisbury and District Preservation Trust 1982 that the summer house was of an earlier date, circa 1790 and was constructed by a gentleman living at 32 High Street. She stated that he initially built a bridge over to the island which was an extension of his garden which ran down to the side stream. He then built the summer house in 1790 on the island incorporating salvaged pieces from the chantry chapels at Salisbury Cathedral, then being demolished by James Wyatt, the famous Gothic Revival architect. Edna reported that there were blocks of Chilmark stone in the west wall, crenellations, a door, and a very fine section of carved stone set into the ceiling. The late Hugh Shortt, curator of Salisbury

Museum allegedly advised her the carving was from the Beauchamp Chapel at Salisbury Cathedral and previously was coloured, although now white. He felt the carving could be of a 15th century date because of the notches for lances in the sides of the shields. Hugh Shortt allegedly indicated to her he had a photograph of the carving at the Museum. Further research would be required to find out if this photograph still exists.

What can now be seen on the fine plaster ceiling are blank shields, so was more detail seen at the time of his assessment and has the ceiling since deteriorated? Perhaps he was referring to a different section of ceiling altogether now replaced? A current expert on Salisbury Cathedral supports the view that the ceiling in bay E is fine plaster work rather than stone and he feels it does not come from the demolished Beauchamp Chapel at Salisbury Cathedral.[7]

It is possible that the former summer house or at least parts of it are of an earlier date than 1820. The site of 32 High Street once stretched as far back as the banks of the River Avon close to where the island was sited up to the 1980s. A bridge can be seen on the 1854 map over to the island (Fig 3). 32 High Street was a medieval building possibly dating from 1491, which was demolished in 1976. Clearly, it existed in the 18th century and also was known to be a City property up to 1876.[8] An examination of City leases available relating to 32 High Street and neighbouring properties in the 18th and 19th centuries, however, provides no indication on who the gentleman was, responsible for the construction of the summer house.[9] These leases do not refer to the island nor the summer house but both may have been covered by a separate lease, not yet found. It is known from a draft conveyance of 1913, both the island and the summer house were in the same ownership from at least 1886. The contents of the draft conveyance will be referred to again in more detail later.[10]

It is interesting to note the existence of a small building or structure on the island, described as gardens on William Naish's 18th century map of Salisbury (Fig 14).[11] Did some of the materials from this small building, which has not been seen again on later maps, eventually become part of the summer house, now part of 102 Crane Street?

Now turning to the occupation of 102 Crane Street; Edward and Anne Pilbrow were living at 98 Crane Street by the 1861 Census with their daughter Elizabeth and a house servant. Edward was an artist and dealer in pictures. This was before the current 98 and 100 (Masonic Hall) Crane Street were built. This suggests that they lived

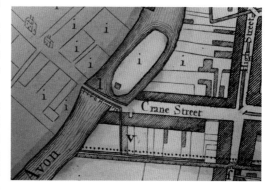

Fig 14 - Extract from the Plan of the City of Salisbury surveyed by William Naish in 1716 and printed in 1751 – showing Crane Street (i - gardens, l - Crane Bridge)

in a property later identified as Retreat Cottage with extensive grounds which probably included the summer house straddling the river. In 1866, Edward Pilbrow made a will in which he was described again as an artist and living at Retreat Cottage.[12]

By the 1871 Census, Matthew and Elizabeth Handford were now occupying 98 Crane Street with their three daughters and a domestic servant. He was a hotel keeper and it is possible that Retreat Cottage was an establishment providing overnight accommodation. Again, the summer house may have been occupied by them.[13] By the 1881 Census, the Handford family were no longer living in Crane Street.

OS maps of Salisbury in the 1880s suggest however that the island and the summer house were now under the same ownership and the association with Retreat Cottage may have ended (Figs 15, 16).[14] The boundary of the Retreat Cottage site appears to run along the now straight south-east elevation of the summer house on the 1880 OS map and the summer house is identified as being in the same ownership as the island on the 1881 OS map.

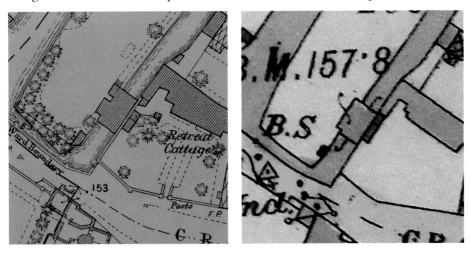

Figs 15 and 16 – Extracts from the 1880 (left) and 1881 (right) OS maps of Salisbury both showing the summer house straddling the River Avon adjacent to Retreat Cottage

The OS map of Salisbury published later in 1887 still shows just the summer house straddling the River Avon adjacent to Retreat Cottage.[15]

Within the draft conveyance dated 1913, already referred to, a schedule of previous deeds shows that the island was sold along with the summer house by James Rawlence to Charles and Frank Luxton in 1886. In 1880, there was a firm of land agents and surveyors called Rawlence, Squarey and Rawlence in Salisbury, whilst the Luxton Brothers were boot and shoe makers on the east side of the High Street.[16]

Edna Trott also recollected in 1982, that the summer house became stabling for Sir George Meyrick, when he was visiting Salisbury from his estate in the country. It is likely she is referring to Sir George Tapp-Meyrick, 3rd Baronet (1827-1896), who was a landowner with estates at Hinton Admiral in Dorset and in Anglesey.[17] Possibly he rented the stabling from the Luxton brothers.

The schedule of previous deeds also shows that the island was sold again with the summer house by Charles and Frank Luxton to Thomas Scamell in 1900. Thomas Scamell was keen to improve access to the island and an agreement was struck with the New Sarum's Urban Sanitary Authority in 1900 to allow the construction of a private bridge over to the island from the Crane Street entrance, including the widening of the entrance and erection of new entrance gates for a charge of five shillings a year. It is clear from the agreement that Thomas Scamell owned the land and buildings on the site of 102 Crane Street. An extract from the plan accompanying the agreement can be seen in Fig 17.

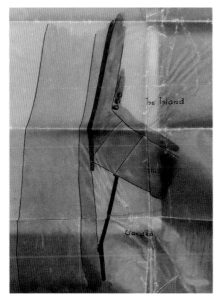 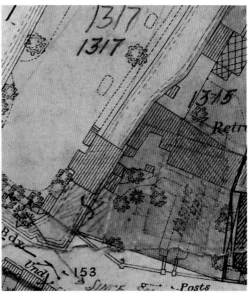

Fig 17 (left) Extract from plan annexed to the agreement between Thomas Scamell and the New Sarum's Urban Sanitary Authority made on 19 July 1900
Fig 18 (right) Extract from the Inland Revenue Survey map - Salisbury dated 1910 focussing on Crane Street near Crane Bridge (No 1317 in the ownership of Frank Watson, No 1315 in the ownership of the freemasons)

There is a shed (coloured grey) located next to the proposed private bridge (coloured brown), which was then a simple roofed structure also now straddling the river, adjacent to the summer house. This structure did not appear on the OS map of 1887, so it is likely it was put in place between 1887 and 1900 by the Luxton brothers. It was probably a commercial building, with few details. Later it was merged into the other buildings on the 102 Crane Street site.

The private bridge was constructed, although not in place in time to appear on the OS map of Salisbury published in 1901 (Fig 5).

In 1902, the schedule of previous deeds indicates that Thomas Scamell sold the island and the unoccupied buildings to Edward Wilkes Gawthorne. He was a hotel proprietor and an ironmonger living at 77 Castle Street.[18] The schedule of deeds, also show he then sold on the island and the site of 102 Crane Street to Frank Watson in 1904. At this point, the island was still being described as a garden and the building on the 102 Crane Street site as a summer house. Frank Watson was a china and glass merchant living at 15 Canal Street.[19]

During this period from 1900 to 1904, Retreat Cottage was demolished to make way for the Masonic Hall. The transition can be seen on the Inland Revenue map of 1910, which is based on the OS map of 1880. The island and buildings straddling the river were still in the ownership of Frank Watson in 1910 (Fig 18).[20]

By 1925, it is clear that further buildings had been constructed on the island. Also, the footprint of the building on the 102 Crane Street site had expanded and consisted of three distinct sections and its footprint was closer to how it is today. Further to this, the new bridge to the island can be seen.[21]

Edna Trott stated that the summer house had been a stable but then became three lock-up garages, and the one facing the pavement was rented for many years by Mr Holland-Young of the Old George Hotel, 'to house his beautiful yellow motor-car'. Archive documents have been found that show his association with 'The George Hotel' between 1926 and 1942.[22] It appears that the roughly triangular building added on the east side was the garage rented by Mr Holland-Young. Around this time, the west wall may also have been rebuilt in line with the original summer house west wall, so increasing the space for use as another garage.

From 1935 to 1945, electoral registers show that the site of 102 Crane Street, along with other buildings on the island were either still in use as garages or were being used for other non-residential purposes.[23] Correspondence between the City engineer and the Avon & Stour Catchment Board in 1936 indicates that Frank Watson was still the owner of the island and the site of 102 Crane Street in that year.[24]

As early as 1936-7, Salisbury Corporation was considering the widening of the main waterway on the west side of the island and the purchase of the site in order to effect the necessary improvements. However, nothing actually happened in this regard until the early 1980s.[25]

In her recollections published in 1982, Edna Trott indicated that 102 Crane Street became an art shop in 1953-4. This explains the different sectioning of the building showing on the OS map of 1953 (Fig 5).[26] Along with the building being re-fronted for a shop, this is the likely time when there was a change to the roofline with the addition of a softwood mono pitch roof covered in corrugated asbestos.

Edna Trott recollected in 1954 finding traces in the building of a charming wallpaper with huge pale yellow roses trailing over a duck-egg blue background.

A Salisbury trade directory of 1956 confirms that Edna Trott was running a specialist art shop known as The Compleat Artist in that year and she was living opposite at 2 Diocesan Church House in Crane Street.[27]

Edna Trott remembered years later, when a second garage was incorporated into the shop, a corroded but unexploded hand-grenade was found, and it transpired that this garage had been used as a Home Guard post during the Second World War. The Sarum City Company of the Wiltshire Home Guard had a headquarters at 89 Crane Street.[28]

A letter of complaint to the Corporation about the Crane Bridge reconstruction in 1970 made on behalf of Edna Trott shows she continued to run The Compleat Artist until at least 1970.[29] By 1972, the shop had changed hands and then again in 1980, when Martyn Kennard and his wife Victoria took over the running of the business.[30] Martyn Kennard continued to run The Compleat Artist until his death in March 2013.

The *Salisbury Journal* reporting his death on 16th April 2013 stated:

'Well known for painting the Crane Street store in a range of vibrant colours (he worked his way through the colour spectrum), he enjoyed creating a little controversy and was delighted when a bright purple shade caused a stir in the city.'

Following Martyn Kennard's death, his three daughters continued to run the business, with his youngest daughter, Lydia in charge. Sadly, the three sisters, none of whom lived in Salisbury, found it too difficult to continue the business and it was reported in the *Salisbury Journal* on 19th January 2015 that The Compleat Artist had stopped trading.[31]

Since the closure of The Compleat Artist in 2015, the former art shop has remained closed and boarded up. However, planning permission was applied for in June 2015 to repair the culvert section under the building and since then a change of ownership has occurred.

We wait to see what the future holds for the former art shop at 102 Crane Street.

## Acknowledgements

Phillip Smith, the current owner, has kindly agreed to the production of this article about 102 Crane Street. I am grateful for the assistance provided by Gerald Steer, an architect in Salisbury who was the author of the article 'The Art Shop by Crane Bridge' containing the recollections of Miss Edna Trott, which appeared in the 1982 newsletter of the Salisbury and District Preservation Trust. I would like to thank Howard Jones, architect, now retired, for his opinion on the ceiling above the former bay window. All photographs of the building and related archive material have been taken by the WBR. All archive documents photographed by the WBR are reproduced by kind permission of the Wiltshire & Swindon History Centre.

## Bibliography

Hall, Linda, *Period House, Fixtures & Fittings 1300 -1900,* 2005, Countryside Books

Royal Commission on Historical Monuments (England), 1980, *Ancient and Historical Monuments in the City of Salisbury, Volume 1,* Her Majesty's Stationery Office, London

## Notes

1 Wiltshire Buildings Record, Wiltshire and Swindon History Centre, The Compleat Artist, 102 Crane Street, Salisbury, Heritage Statement prepared by D Treasure & L Purdy May 2016 - B17731

2 Steer, Gerald, 1982, 'The Art Shop by Crane Bridge', Salisbury and District Preservation Trust newsletter, back page

3 Wiltshire and Swindon Archives (WSA), G23/701/1PC, Salisbury City Council, Local Board of Health plan of City's sewerage and drainage scheme (26 maps in bound volume), sheet 16, 1854

4 1861 Census RG 09/1316 f12

5 WSA, OS map of Salisbury 1901 (25 inch), sheet 66/15, OS map of Salisbury 1925 (25 inch), sheet 66/15 and OS map of Salisbury 1953 (1:2500), Plan SU 1429

6 Hall, Linda, *Period House, Fixtures & Fittings 1300 -1900* p49 – a very similar strap hinge from Surrey has been dated to 1598, p33 – whilst the door resembles another example dated 1634 from Sussex. The drop loop handle with decorative back plate matches several 17th century examples identified by Linda Hall pp54-56

7 Tim Tatton-Brown, consultant archaeologist at Salisbury Cathedral referred Dorothy Treasure in regard to the ceiling to Howard Jones, independent consultant and architect (now retired), with extensive experience of working on projects relating to Salisbury Cathedral. Howard Jones was of the view that the section of ceiling found in Bay E was of plaster rather than stone and he did not believe that the ceiling came from the Beauchamp Chapel at Salisbury Cathedral.

8 Royal Commission on Historical Monuments (England), 1980, *Ancient and Historical Monuments in the City of Salisbury, Volume 1,* 'High Street' pp 66-72

9 WSA, Houses bounded by High Street on east and River Avon on west – 1438 -1853 (City Lands)

10 WSA, G23/150/121, Salisbury City Council, Deeds – Island used as garden in River Avon between Fisherton and Crane Bridges, 1900-1913, Draft Conveyance of a portion of 'The Island' situate in Crane Street, Salisbury Wilts – 3rd December 1913

11  WSA, G23/1/164PC, Salisbury City Council - Printed plan of City surveyed by William Naish (original and 2 copies) 1751

12  WSA, Salisbury Probate Registry, Register of Wills , P31/1/15/59 - Edward Pilbrow, Artist, Retreat Cottage, Crane Street, Salisbury, 1872

13  1871 Census RG 10/1953 f14

14  WSA, OS map of Salisbury 1880 First Edition (1:500 scale), sheet 66. 15.3  and OS map of Salisbury 1881 (25 inch), sheet 66/15

15  WSA, OS map of Salisbury 1887 (6 inch), sheet 66

16  Wiltshire Local Studies Library - Kelly's Directory of Hampshire, Wiltshire and Dorsetshire, 1880

17  http://www.historyofparliamentonline.org/volume/1820-1832/member/tapps-george-1795-1842 [accessed March 2017]

18  1901 Census RG 13/1954 f42

19  1901 Census RG 13/1954 f13

20  WSA, L8/1/166, L8/1/167 and L8/10/66 (map) - Inland Revenue Survey 1910, Salisbury

21  WSA, OS map of Salisbury 1925 (25 inch), sheet 66/15

22  WSA, 182/21, Architectural Records, Public Houses - Old George Hotel, High Street, Salisbury. W. Holland-Young 1926 -1942

23  WSA, Electoral Registers for Salisbury 1925, 1935, 1936 and 1945

24  WSA, G23/742/4, Salisbury City Council - Avon and Stour River Board 1932-1954

25  WSA,  G23/742/4,  Salisbury City Council, Avon and Stour River Board 1932-1954

26  WSA, OS map of Salisbury 1953 (1:2500 scale), Plan SU 1429

27  Wiltshire Local Studies Library, Kelly's Directory of Salisbury and neighbourhood dated 1956

28  http://www.wiltshirehomeguard.co.uk [accessed 13 March 2017]

29  WSA, G23/742/44, Salisbury City Council - Crane Bridge Reconstruction 1969-73

30  SJ 16 April 2013

31  SJ 19 January 2015

Fig 1. de Cort's drawing of St Thomas's Church, with modern view (Roy Bexon)

# Hendrick de Cort's drawings of Salisbury

## Tim Tatton-Brown and Jane Howells

The Flemish artist, Hendrick Josef Frans de Cort was born in Antwerp on 11 December 1742. He studied and worked there until the later 1770s, when he spent some time in Paris. Returning to Antwerp he was one of the founders of a group of artists called 'Konstmaatschappij' (the 'Art Society') in 1781. Around 1790, and probably because of the wars in Europe, he moved to London where he made his home until his death on 28 June 1810.[1]

In England and Wales de Cort became widely known as a draughtsman and painter of topographical views, particularly of castles, cathedrals, and country houses. He built up a network of patrons by personal recommendation and word of mouth; for example Arthur Champernowne, of Dartington Hall and briefly MP for Saltash in Cornwall, wrote to the artist Ozias Humphrey in July 1794 saying he was sorry not to be able to stay in Bristol 'to meet Mr de Cort who hopes to tour the west country in the summer. He has recommended him to some of his friends'.[2]

De Cort's growing popularity entailed extensive travels around the country to fulfil commissions. While on these journeys he also undertook detailed views of townscapes such as the four of Salisbury illustrated and discussed here. He worked on preparatory wash drawings in the field, and often produced the finished oil paintings on mahogany panels. Many were exhibited at the Royal Academy and the British Institution, the first at the RA in 1790. In 1797 both 'Salisbury Cathedral' and 'St Thomas's, Salisbury' appeared there.[3]

When the British Institution held its first exhibition in 1806, Henry de Cort exhibited three paintings including Kenilworth Castle, and Carphilly (*sic*) Castle.[4] The organisation's full title was 'for promoting the Fine Arts in the United Kingdom' with the aim 'to encourage the talents of the Artists of the United Kingdom' suggesting that by that time de Cort was accepted into

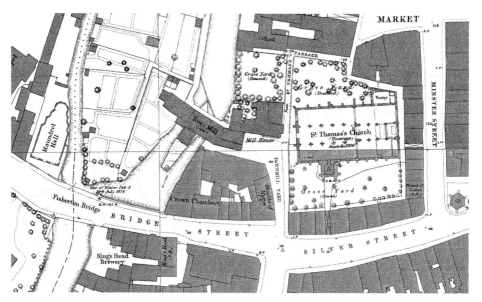

The area of St Thomas's Church shown on Ordnance Survey 1:500 plan of Salisbury 1880-1, sheets (clockwise beginning top left) 66.11.23, 66.11.24, 66.15.4, 66.15.3.

artistic circles of his adopted country, as well as anglicising his first name.[5]

Major paintings by de Cort can now be found in the houses of the National Trust, English Heritage, and the National Museum of Wales. Quantities of his drawings are in collections at the British Museum, and the Ashmolean, Oxford. His 'A view of Windsor Castle' is at Longford Castle.[6]

The Salisbury Museum has five of his drawings. A view of Salisbury Cathedral from the bishop's grounds (apparently dated 1795)[7] and four other less-well-known pencil sketches shown here.[8] It is possible that these were carried out while de Cort was in the area to paint Fonthill Splendens for William Beckford, though he did other work in the area, such as Charlton Park in north Wilts in c1800.[9]

The first of these (Fig 1) which is very accurately drawn, is a view east-south-east across the millstream to St Thomas's Church. It can be compared with T Langley's engraved view of the church from the north-west in 1745, on John Lyon's plan.[10] The north porch, demolished in 1835, is shown with a chamber above, and behind it the three-storied late 15th century clergy house, now the vestry. When the north porch was knocked down in 1835, the graveyard was enlarged westwards to the millstream, so the interesting building behind the wall, with a tower, must also have been demolished at this time. It is however shown on Naish's map of c1716,[11] as a tower arch, and this was probably part of *Vine Inn*, the 17th century (and earlier) house belonging to William Vyner, vintner. The building became property of the Dean & Chapter in 1795, as part of an

Fig 2. de Cort's drawing of the Town Mill, with modern view (Roy Bexon)

exchange for the new Guildhall.[12] On the extreme right of the drawing is the still-existing north-east corner of the Town Mill, which was rebuilt in 1757.[13]

This mill is also shown from the south-west in the second of de Cort's drawings (Fig 2). This view, which is looking east, shows the tower of St Thomas's in the background, and the south-west front of the 1757 mill, and its timber-framed south-west extension between the sluices. To the right is the complex of buildings that were apparently the *London Inn*.[14] This area was rebuilt in the mid-19th century as Crown Chambers (now used by Fletchers Accountants). Just out of the view to the right is Fisherton Bridge, which had been rebuilt in 1762 (and again in 1872 and 1960). This bridge must have been one of the original large 13th-century bridges which Leland says had six stone arches.[15]

The third view by de Cort (Fig 3) is more difficult to locate. However the cathedral's tower and spire, at an angle of 45°, is in the background, and the view is almost certainly from the north-west. The artist must therefore have been in Fisherton Street near Summerlock Bridge. The large area of water in the foreground is probably part of a ford on Fisherton Street (the Naish map shows only a very small bridge here), and beyond one can see various properties with doors in the wall (and privies) on the river. Some of these can still be seen in Water Lane today. The stream here is a back branch of the Avon, which must have originated with the tail drains of the watermeadows west of the Avon, as shown on the early Ordnance Survey maps. In the later 19th century much of the southern part of this area was overrun by railway lines and malthouses. The 'Summerlock' was presumably the sluice near the Avon, which was opened to dry out the meadows for the haycrop after the Spring drownings had ceased.

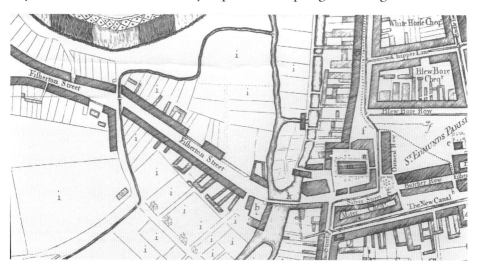

St Thomas's Church (m), the Town Mills(r) and Fisherton Street showing a very narrow Summerlock Bridge, from the map of Salisbury by William Naish, revised edition 1751.

Fig 3. de Cort's drawing near Summerlock Bridge, with modern view (Roy Bexon)

Fig 4. de Cort's drawing of the river Bourne and Milford Mill Bridge

The final drawing by de Cort (Fig 4) is of the river Bourne and Milford Mill Bridge looking east. Almost a mile away, and also very carefully drawn, is the east end, and tower and spire of Salisbury Cathedral. Just to its left the spire of St Martin's Church can be seen. Unfortunately this view is no longer visible, not just because of modern housing, but also because so many large trees have grown up in the area. Even the fine medieval bridge with its two pairs of arches connected by a parapetted causeway is now mostly obscured by vegetation. The bridge, which was perhaps first built in the 12th century and then rebuilt in the later Middle Ages, no doubt because it was for the main access road to Clarendon, has yet to be studied archaeologically. The two western arches are over the River Bourne, while those to the east went over the man-made milltail for Milford Mill. The river is the original eastern boundary of the City of New Sarum, with the mill lying outside it, in Laverstock. Just beyond this were many medieval pottery and tile-kilns,[16] though their products must have been taken in carts to Salisbury across the eponymous Milford, which was clearly on the south side of the bridge, and in the area shown in the foreground of de Cort's drawing. It is also worth noting that John Constable sketched a distant view of the cathedral, with the eastern approach to Milford Bridge, in July 1820. This must have been taken from only a few yards north of de Cort's viewpoint. An engraving of this view was made in 1826, as well as a beautiful small watercolour in 1836.[17]

This informative and under-appreciated set of drawings of late 18th century Salisbury make a valuable contribution to our knowledge of the city's townscape at the time.

## Acknowledgements:

de Cort drawings reproduced by kind permission of The Salisbury Museum; modern photographs by Roy Bexon.

## Notes

1  Biographical information from Grove Art Online accessed 18 February 2017
2  Royal Academy archive HU/4/98 www/racollection.org
3  Graves, Algernon, 1905-6, *The Royal Academy of Arts A Complete Dictionary of Contributors and their Work from its Foundation in 1769 to 1904*, 291. Online Hathi Trust Digital Library accessed 19 March 2017
4  Graves, Algernon, 1908, *The British Institution 1806-1867 A Complete Dictionary of Contributors and Their Work from the Foundation of the Institution*, 151. Online Hathi Trust Digital Library accessed 19 March 2017
5  Smith, Thomas, MDCCCLX, *Recollections of the Rise and progress of the British Institution*, 4. Googlebooks online accessed 19 March 2017
6  http://openiart.uk/object/?ID=123618  accessed 27 April 2017
7  Wilcox, T, 2011, *Constable and Salisbury, the soul of landscape*, 88-90. Constable's famous view of the cathedral from the bishop's grounds, first made in 1811, is taken from beyond the canal a little further to the south-west.
8  These were purchased in 1996 'Four late 18th century sepia watercolour drawings by Henri (*sic*) de Cort. 43/1996. Salisbury & South Wiltshire Museum, *Annual Report 1996-97*, 24.
9  A number of drawings of Fonthill, dated between 1791 and 1798, were sold at Christies in 2013 (Sale 1137 www.christies.com). See also www.fonthill.co.uk/fonthill-history. The picture of Charlton Park is in its Wikipedia entry.
10 Fig 2 in Tatton-Brown, 1997, 'The church of St Thomas of Canterbury, Salisbury', *Wiltshire Archaeological Magazine* 90, 101-9
11 See Rogers K H (1963) note on the map *WAM* 58, 453-4
12 Royal Commission on Historical Monuments (England) (RCHM) (1980) *City of Salisbury*, vol 1, 61, no 37
13 RCHM (1980) 65, No 66
14 RCHM (1980) No 67
15 See *Victoria County History, Wilts* (1962) Vol VI, 87, for its history.
16 See Musty J et al (1969), 'The medieval pottery kilns at Laverstock near Salisbury Wilts', *Archaeologia* cii, 83-150.
17 Wilcox, 2011, 52, figs 35 and 36

Hannam Edward Bonner, born 1879, changed his named to Albany Ward in 1901. Reproduced by permission of the family of Albany Ward.

# Albany Ward
# Cinema Pioneer of Salisbury

## Ruth Butler

If you want to see the latest movie release in Salisbury you will head for the city's only cinema, the *Odeon*. A hundred years ago there were three picture houses to choose from and the city was at the heart of the country's largest cinema circuit.

Today's *Odeon*, in New Canal, is the only Grade 1 listed cinema in England that is still in use as a film theatre – the others have turned to live theatre or bingo. It has a rather splendid mock Tudor façade which hides an amazing medieval hall, the Hall of John Halle. Beyond that is the 1930s (Grade II listed) building that now houses the modern five-screen cinema.

The cinema was designed by William Edward Trent, chief architect for Provincial Cinematograph Theatres (PCT), which in 1929 was taken over by Gaumont British Picture Corporation. Albany Ward, the name that was synonymous with cinemas and variety theatres in Salisbury and the south west for almost half a century, was associated with the *Odeon*, when it was known as the *Gaumont Palace*.

Albany Ward was an ambitious young man who in the late 1890s recognised that the latest craze for moving pictures was not just a passing fad. By the time his name became associated with the *Gaumont*, Albany Ward no longer owned the cinema circuit he had built up over 20 years. Albany Ward Theatres Ltd was sold in 1921 but the name lived on for another 30 years and remained connected to cinemas and theatres across the region, including the *Gaumont* in Salisbury.

Albany Ward was one of the pioneers who laid the foundations for today's cinema conglomerates that dominate our film-going experiences today. I first came across him in early 2014 when I was education officer at The Salisbury Museum. His daughter Jean Thorpe got in touch having heard a radio interview I had given asking for people to contribute Home Front stories for the museum's Great War centenary exhibition.[1]

Jean explained that her father had owned and operated three cinemas in Salisbury, had moved his business headquarters to the city in 1913, and when the First World War broke out, he quickly established a mobile cinema circuit serving the many military camps in Wiltshire and further afield.

When I visited Jean she showed me three marvellous scrapbooks full of letters, envelopes, autographs and press cuttings which her father had collected. There were also autobiographical notes he had written in his later years and which included a description of his work during the war.

It was clear there was a great story to be told. For the purposes of the Museum's exhibition I focused on Ward's activities from 1914-18 and the cinemas he established to entertain the many thousands of troops who descended on Wiltshire to train for battle. Jean kindly allowed the Museum to reproduce family photographs and loaned one of his scrapbooks containing letters relating to his war-time business, including correspondence with senior army officers from Southern Command based in Radnor House, Salisbury.

From 1914-18 Albany Ward operated a mobile cinema and theatre circuit to entertain the troops training on Salisbury Plain. Reproduced by permission of the family of Albany Ward.

There was further information that I could not include in the 2014 exhibition, but when I moved to the Wiltshire and Swindon History Centre I had the opportunity to do more research and reach new audiences.

From my discussion with Jean it was clear that her father had a pioneering and entrepreneurial, if rather restless, spirit. He was born in Stoke Newington on 6th November 1879 and christened Hannam Edward Bonnor. He was educated at Christ's Hospital in the City of London (before its move to Horsham, Sussex in

Albany Ward trained as a projectionist, also known as a lanternist, and set up his own business in 1898. Reproduced by permission of the family of Albany Ward.

1902) and family accounts of his time at the boarding school recall a spartan regime where the young Hannam would often go hungry. In 1891 he appears on the school's census return; his parents wcrc living in Hampstead where his father was retired.

A decade later and Hannam Edward Bonnor disappeared from census returns and instead appears as Albany Ward, occupation 'theatrical manager'. The 1901 census shows him living in Cowley Road, Oxford, with his first wife May (Edith May Robertson) who was an operatic vocalist.[2]

By 1901 Albany Ward had been working in the burgeoning film industry for five years. In 1896 he had gone to work for one of the great innovators in English film-making, Birt Acres. The young Hannam had met Acres by chance while on a family holiday in 1893 and three years later, having left school, he went to work for Acres in north London.

Albany Ward spent a year with Acres, a year in which Acres invented a successful film projector before moving to the Velograph Company in 1897. It was here that Ward trained to be a lanternist (projectionist) and began touring the country with the short films that were being made at that time, including film of Queen Victoria's diamond jubilee.

While Acres was technically adept he did not possess the business acumen of Albany Ward who saw the potential in entertaining audiences with films.[3] In 1898 Ward bought his first film projector and set up his own business touring the south and west exhibiting films. In autobiographical notes written in the mid-1940s he noted: 'In the early days, particularly in the early 1900s, I can well recollect that the majority of important people in the theatrical business laughed at those of us who thought that there was a future for the cinema and I can well remember the late Mr George Edwardes telling me personally that it was quite hopeless and that the Cinema would be dead within a year or two if it lasted as long as that.'[4]

As a travelling projectionist Albany Ward was used to showing films in all sorts of venues – shops, fairgrounds, local halls – and some were considerably

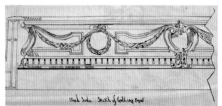

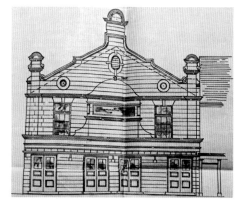

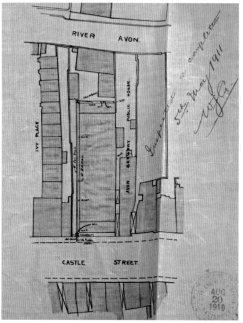

*left, top and above:* Architect's drawings from 1914 for the internal decoration of the new *Picture Theatre* in Trowbridge. (Wiltshire & Swindon History Centre WSA 1451/26HC)

*right, top and above:* The 1910 plans for the *New Theatre* on Castle Street in Salisbury show its location next to the Avon Brewery (Wiltshire & Swindon History Centre G23/760/23)

more salubrious than others. While film-making improved and camera and projector technology advanced, the existence of good quality venues for showing films was distinctly lacking, perhaps not surprising given the attitude of theatre managers like George Edwardes. Looking at the planning applications made by Ward for conversions and new builds it is clear he wanted his picture palaces to be just that – palatial and aspirational.

Albany Ward opened his first permanent picture house in 1909 in Weymouth, where he was living, and in 1911 the census records his occupation as 'proprietor of theatres and skating rinks etc'. His first cinema in Salisbury was on the corner of Endless Street and Chipper Lane; it was renamed the *Palace Theatre* in 1910. That year he applied for planning permission for a purpose-built theatre in Castle Street and this opened in 1911 as the *New Theatre*.

At this time many of the new cinemas springing up in towns and cities were theatres or spacious buildings that could be converted to accommodate large audiences as well as the projection room and screen. Albany Ward's third Salisbury cinema was just such a building – the Methodist hall in Fisherton Street which was transformed in 1916 into the *Picture House*.

Weymouth remained home to Albany Ward for two more years until 1913 when he moved the headquarters of his rapidly expanding cinema circuit to Salisbury, setting up headquarters at Weymouth House.[5] By this time the circuit comprised 26 theatres in towns across Wiltshire, Somerset, Dorset, the Channel Islands and South Wales, and in the year of his move to Salisbury he opened the *Palladium* in Exeter.[6]

As well as the picture palaces Ward also ran a film renting company – Award Film Services – which had offices off Wardour Street in London. Not content with owning and operating the cinema and film businesses, he also established a printing firm which he renamed Salisbury Press when he moved to the city.

By 1914 Salisbury residents were spoilt for entertainment choice; not only could they see the latest films, there was an ever-changing programme of music hall and variety acts. On the eve of the outbreak of the First World War, adverts in the *Salisbury Journal* show the *New Theatre* in Castle Street focusing on plays and

These adverts for Albany Ward's theatres ran on 1st August 1914, just three days before Britain declared war on Germany. (Author's own photos.)

comedy theatre while the *Palace Theatre* in Endless Street had film shows and variety acts.

Albany Ward was now the owner and operator of the largest cinema circuit in the country having added another three theatres to the 26 he ran in 1913. The next largest company was Provincial Cinematograph Theatres (18 picture houses) which would eventually buy out Ward. Film theatres were hugely popular by 1914 and while there were thousands of cinemas around the country there were only 109 circuits which ran multiple venues, and only a handful of those with 10 or more cinemas.[7]

"The Palace." Codford-St-Peter.

Within two days of war being declared Albany Ward had opened *The Palace* cinema in Codford. The village's population of around 200 exploded overnight with the arrival of more than 20,000 soldiers. Photo *c*1914. Reproduced by permission of the family of Albany Ward.

Just as Albany Ward recognised in 1898 that the new world of film could be big business he knew with equal certainty in August 1914 that the thousands of soldiers heading to Salisbury Plain to train for war would need entertaining. 'When war was declared, . . . I was of course at Salisbury which was my Headquarters and I at once decided to offer my services to the War Department, and I approached General Pitcairn Campbell who was in charge of the Southern Command and offered to put up and open a proper Cinema Theatre in Codford for the benefit of the Troops who were drafted there immediately, including the famous Black Watch with the result I opened the *Palace*, Codford, within two days of war being declared and we actually opened the same night that the original men of the Black Watch arrived in camp.'[8]

Ward went on to open cinemas in military camps across the Southern Command area, including Larkhill, Fovant, Hurdcott, Sutton Veny, Heytesbury and two at Bulford. He established a mobile cinema and theatre circuit arranging films and variety acts to be staged for the soldiers' entertainment. He wrote: 'For this I built up a special organisation including our own motor transport as we ran not only Pictures but Variety Turns with a proper stage fitted with scenery, and electric light generated by our own plant at all these Theatres, which were completely equipped with Tip-up seating, central heating and every convenience that could be provided. In fact, I think I can justly say that my Theatres were the most comfortable buildings in the respective camps and the Troops were only too glad to go to them at night, knowing they would be warm and comfortable.' [9]

As the war progressed he struggled to keep staff as they went off to enlist or were later called up. He also feared being called up himself as replies to letters he wrote to Southern Command Headquarters at Radnor House in Salisbury confirm.

In 1915 volunteer enlistment slowed down and in the autumn of that year the government introduced the Derby scheme to ensure the military's manpower needs were met. Men aged 18 to 41 were told to report to their local recruiting office where they would enlist and be placed in the army reserve to be called up at a later date. Single men were to be called up before married men. Certain jobs were also protected if considered essential to the war effort.

Ward wrote to Southern Command in 1915 and received the following reply on 3rd November 1915 from Lieutenant General Pitcairn Campbell, the General Officer Commanding-in-Chief: 'I am of the opinion that in helping to entertain the men in various camps around Salisbury and in Salisbury itself, Mr Albany Ward is doing great work for the nation and I consider that he should be relieved from service with the Colours. He is giving every facility for his staff to enlist.' [10]

In 1916 conscription was introduced and in March 1917 Ward again sought written assurances that he would not be called up. In reply Colonel F Wintour of Southern Command wrote: '... The major general i/c administration authorises me to say that he regards it of great importance that the troops should have attractive and wholesome places of recreation at hand in their camps, and that he has no hesitation in acknowledging the value of the work you are carrying on, the utility of which is fully appreciated at Command Headquarters.' [11]

Despite these preoccupations, Albany Ward not only kept both civilian and military cinema circuits going with packed programmes of the latest films and music hall and variety acts, he also got married for a second time and opened a new venue in Salisbury. [12]

In December 1916, despite growing restrictions on building materials, Ward opened the *Picture House* in Fisherton Street amid much fanfare and publicity in the local press. The *Salisbury Times and South Wilts Gazette* described the

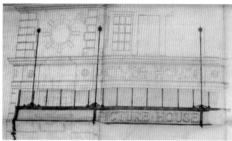

*above:* Fisherton Street in 1928 with Albany Ward's *Picture House* on the left. (copyright The Francis Frith Collection)

*left:* This architect's drawing shows the detail of the façade when planning permission for the *Picture House* was sought in 1915. (Wiltshire & Swindon History Centre G23/760/147)

600-seater cinema as 'Salisbury's new hall of delight' ahead of its opening on 11th December. The newspaper also reported that £7,000 had been spent on converting the old Methodist hall '… and a pleasing feature of the work is that it is practically the outcome of local talent.' As well as local architects and builders, Salisbury's premiere department store Style and Gerrish did the upholstery while Albany Ward drafted in his own staff to complete the decorating. The advert for the grand opening styled the *Picture House* as a 'Beautifully-appointed and Up-to-date Cinema de Luxe'. [13]

The advert also highlighted another aspect of Ward's life – his generosity to charities. He announced that the entirety of the opening day's box office receipts would go the mayor's fund for Salisbury Infirmary. Giving generous donations to charity was characteristic of her father according to Jean Thorpe.

December 1916 also saw the return to Albany Ward's theatres of the film that had the nation transfixed earlier in the year, *The Battle of the Somme*. The film was first shown at the *New Theatre* in Castle Street at the beginning of October: three showings a day for three days and all were sold out. This prompted an extra showing at the *Palace Theatre*. Such was the demand to see the film it returned to Salisbury for a further three days in the run-up to Christmas.

Twenty years after first venturing into the film industry Ward dominated the regional cinema scene in the south west. He also ran his printing business, Salisbury Press, based in Wilton Road, and in London (he had) his film rental business, Award Film Service.[14]

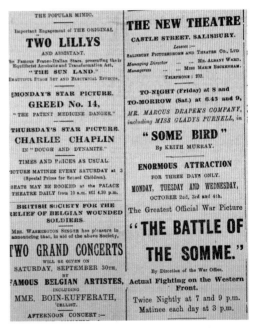

*left:* An advert from the *Salisbury Times and South Wilts Gazette* of 8th December 1916 announcing the gala opening of the Fisherton Street *Picture House*.
*right:* In October 1916 the *New Theatre* and *Palace Theatre* had shown the Battle of the Somme film to sell-out houses. Albany Ward brought the film back to Salisbury for a further three days just before Christmas 1916. (Author's own photos)

So why at the end of the war was Albany Ward not competing with PCT and Gaumont to dominate the national cinema landscape?

In 1918 the military authorities decided to take direct control of camp entertainment for the troops. Ward recalled being offered a Commission in the Army to allow him to continue running his circuit of military cinemas but he declined: '… I did not feel disposed to accept this appointment, feeling that

I would prefer to remain independent . . .' He still had his original circuit of theatres but an accident changed everything. 'Unfortunately I met with a very serious accident in December 1918 which nearly killed me with the result that I was incapacitated for nearly 12 months and it was then that I decided to sell my cinema circuit...' [15]

The next largest circuit after Albany Ward's was *PCT* and in post war Britain it emerged as the first national cinema circuit. Albany Ward recalled that '... although they intended to run it themselves, they subsequently asked me to remain and manage it for them, which I did until 1924, and the Albany Ward Theatres Ltd. which was the subsidiary of PCT proved one of their most profitable investments and I don't think that company has ever experienced a losing week.' [16]

But the world of film was changing rapidly. There was money to be invested and made from film production and exhibition, especially after 'talkies' arrived in Britain in 1928. Benefiting from this growth was Gaumont British Picture Corporation which acquired PCT and its subsidiaries in 1929. By 1931 Gaumont had opened yet another cinema in Salisbury – the *Gaumont Palace*. The company's expansion did not stop there. In 1937 Albany Ward's original *Picture House* in Fisherton Street closed to make way for Gaumont's thousand-seater *New Picture Palace* which was built next door. Actress Nova Pilbeam (who starred in two Alfred Hitchcock films) was the star attraction at the gala opening on 27th September 1937 but one of the honoured guests was Albany Ward.

Although his connection with his namesake company ended in 1924, Albany Ward Theatres Ltd carried on in business until it was finally wound up in April 1951.

His printing business in Salisbury continued and he ventured into property development, building a number of houses in Hulse Road. While Salisbury remained home to his business interests he was not permanently resident in the city. In the 1930s he appears on the Stroud (Gloucestershire) electoral roll while ships' passenger lists show he was resident in Torquay in 1948 and Weymouth in 1954. And it was in Torquay that he died, aged 86, on 18th February 1966.

Today, sadly, Albany Ward's picture palaces have gone – demolished and forgotten – but the next time you go to the movies remember that the foundations of today's cinema industry in England were built in Salisbury.

## Notes

1   Salisbury Museum's First World War centenary exhibition – *Salisbury & The Great War: Fighting on the Home Front* – ran from October 2014 to January 2015. It was co-curated by Ruth Butler and local historian Ken Smith, and designed by Kim Chittick.

2   Although he appears on the census as Albany Ward, legal documents referred to him as Hannam Edward Bonnor until 1922 when he finally and formally changed his name by

deed poll. The 1901 census shows other anomalies – his age is recorded as 30, and his wife is 25. We know that Albany Ward was born in 1879 and that when he married in 1899 the marriage certificate records he was 20 and his wife was 25.

3   Birt Acres's biography from the *screenonline, British Film Institute's (BFI)* online history of cinema, recounts both the technical firsts he achieved and also his business failures.

4   George Edwardes was a leading figure in theatre management and production in the late 18th and early 19th centuries. His theatres included the *Gaiety* and he was responsible for popularising musical comedy and introducing the 'Gaiety Girls'.

5   Weymouth House, Salisbury is given as Albany Ward's business address and notes from my conversation with Jean Thorpe record her saying these headquarters were in Fisherton Street.

6   Albany Ward's own notes and a listing in the *Kinematograph Year Book 1914* (which reported on the film industry for 1913) show that he had cinemas in Weymouth (4), Jersey (2), Guernsey, Salisbury (3), Yeovil (2), Treharris in south Wales (2), Chippenham, Trowbridge, Warminster, Westbury, Radstock, Blandford, Portland (2), Weston Super Mare, Frome, Wells, and Exeter.

7   Figures on the number and size of cinema circuits in 1914 collected and cross checked from a range of sources including *Kinematograph Year Books* and www.terramedia.co.uk.

8   This quote comes from Albany Ward's own typescript notes on his life and career as preserved in his scrapbooks held by the family.

9   From Albany Ward's autobiographical notes.

10  Quote from the original letter which was kept by Albany Ward in a collection of scrapbooks now held by the family.

11  Extract from letter written by Colonel F Wintour to Albany Ward. Preserved in Ward's scrapbooks.

12  Albany Ward – still legally Hannam Edward Bonnor – married Dorothy Hembrow in Bristol in September 1916.

13  The *Salisbury Times and South Wilts Gazette* dated 8 December, 1916 carried an advert for the gala opening of the *Picture House* and a detailed article about the conversion and fitting out of the building..

14  Albany Ward had to relocate his film rental company *Award Film Services* to Garrick Street after the original offices were bombed in a 1916 Zeppelin air raid.

15  Extract from Ward's autobiographical notes on his life and career.

16  Patricia Cook, in her article 'Albany Ward and the Development of Cinema Exhibition in Britain' for the journal *Film History*, suggests that the autobiographical notes quoted in this article were made in 1946 in response to a request from Rachael Low who was researching her seven-volume *History of British Film*, first published in 1948.

## Bibliography

British Film Institute, The Kinematograph Year Book, Program, Diary and Directory 1914 pdf download retrieved April 2017 http://www.bfi.org.uk/sites/bfi.org.uk/files/downloads/kinematograph-year-book-program-diary-and-directory-1914-2014-09-18.pdf

British Film Institute BFI Screenonline Retrieved April 2017 http://www.screenonline.org.uk/people/id/449777/

Cook, Patricia, 2008, 'Albany Ward and the Development of Cinema Exhibition in Britain.' Film History Volume 20, No3, 2008. Retrieved January and April 2017 https://business.highbeam.com/138317/article-1G1-193736781/albany-ward-and-development-cinema-exhibition-england

Cinema Theatre Association Retrieved April 2017 http://cinema-theatre.org.uk/uk-cinemas/listed-cinemas/england/

Hall, Neil G M, 2016, Salisbury and The Great War (Pen & Sword)

Who's Who in Victorian Cinema http://www.victorian-cinema.net/ retrieved January 2017

McCarraher, James, 2013, Salisbury City Hall Through The Looking Glass

O'Rourke, Chris, London's Silent Cinemas Retrieved January 2017 http://www.londonssilentcinemas.com/history/

Ostrer, Nigel, Gaumont-British Picture Corporation Ltd. Retrieved January and April 2017 http://www.gaumontbritish.com/

Terra Media, 2004, UK Cinema Circuits 1914-1945 Retrieved April 2017 http://www.terramedia.co.uk/reference/statistics/cinema/cinema_circuits.htm accessed

Wellcome Trust, University of Exeter, Devon Heritage Centre & ESRC, Devon County Mental Hospital http://dcmh.exeter.ac.uk/ retrieved April 2017

# St Andrew's Church of England Aided Primary School, Laverstock: History from 1864–1976

## Sharon Evans

Formal education of children in Laverstock began with the decision in 1832 of Thomas Burgess, Bishop of Salisbury, to purchase land in the village centre from William Finch for a Sunday school. In 1835, the provision was

Old school. Newspaper cutting 1940s. Unknown occasion. From private collection courtesy of Ruth Newman.

re-designated Bishop Burgess's Day School. The deed of 14 August 1835[1] directed that this school was to promote the education of poor children in the parishes of Milford and Laverstock. The plot of 30ft x 30ft housed a brick-built, slate-roofed building with a single classroom, and small porch, and the Dean of the Cathedral and the Archdeacon of Sarum became Trustees. Bishop Burgess made an endowment of £666 invested in consolidated stock to provide income for repairs, insurance, and the teacher's salary.

The deed also directed that subjects to be taught should include 'reading, writing, and cyphering' overseen by the managers, who would arrange provision of books, audit accounts, and regulate admission numbers. The numbers would be decided 'having regard to schoolroom size and state of funds', and residence in the parishes of Milford or Laverstock. Milford residents would have priority of admission. Masters or mistresses were to be 'elected and appointed annually'. They must have been members of the Established Church, assenting to its beliefs and practice, for at least two years prior to appointment. Managers could remove them for 'misbehaviour, inability or other cause, at any time', and could dismiss pupils for misconduct, non-attendance or idleness. Trustees would examine the pupils' learning progress annually.

Fees were charged for each pupil, and the school was eligible for some government grant money, subject to the outcome of official inspections. Inspectors reported on the number of sessions held in the school year (a minimum of 400 was required, with a full day counting as two sessions), attendance and the quality of teaching and premises.[2]

Apart from providing the Trustees, Salisbury Diocese also arranged their own regular inspections, of which there are detailed records from 1874-1889[3] (relating to old and new schools). Comments on the teaching capability of mistresses and paid monitors, syllabus, attendance (including that of the Sunday school) and attainment are included. Early reports comment on the markedly small proportion of boys attending, and how competing schools (in Salisbury), and later, new education legislation were influencing this. Equipment and premises, discipline, pupil ability and engagement were assessed.

From 1883 government inspections repeatedly highlighted the inadequate capacity for present and expected numbers of pupils.[4] In 1887 an official notice from the Council of Education dated 27 June threatened imposition of a School Board for the district 'unless capacity was increased, or arrangements for supplying the deficit were at an advanced stage within the next 6 months'.[5] In response, in December 1887 land was secured at another site in the village, and the founding principles of the new school indicated it was 'for the education of such children and adults or children only of the labouring and manufacturing and other poor classes as shall be resident in or parishioners of the parish of

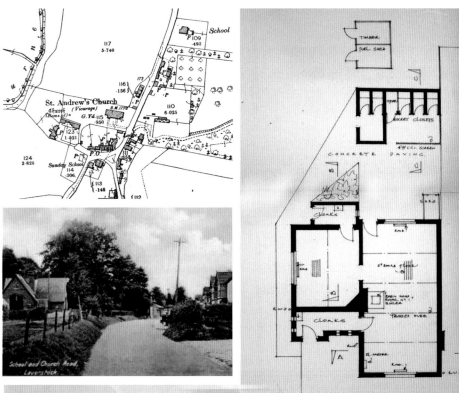

**New school.** *top left:* Ordnance survey map 1901. *centre left:* New school in 1930s from the road (WSA, 1324/56). *bottom left:* New school, unknown date. (courtesy of Mrs K Walker, Headteacher, St Andrew's School). *top right:* Plan of building. June 1960 (WSA, F8/600/169/1/22/1).

Laverstock, and as a residence for teacher(s) of the school'. The school was known as 'Laverstock National School', reflecting its affiliation to the National Society (NS).[6] Trustees' and managers' responsibilities would be unchanged.

The new school (for 85 pupils) with a large and a small classroom and a porch, was officially opened by the Bishop on 2 October 1888. It cost £762 19s 11d, and was built (within his estimate of £770) by H J Kite of 5 Wilton Road, who was also an undertaker.[7] F. Bath, the architect, registered his satisfaction, and the government inspector rated it 'excellent, only needs completion with teacher's house'.[8] This was never built, but 1902 correspondence refers to 'Teacher's house provided … owned by Mr S Parr'.[9]

£754 of the cost of the build was contributed by local private benefactors. Of these, Miss C Everard, who lived at 'The Hall, Laverstock', gave £400 – the largest single donation. Contributions totalling £118 came from the Ecclesiastical Commissioners, the Board of Education, and the National Society.[10]

List of donors, new school (WSA, F8/600/169/1/26/1)

Funding exercised the Trustees and managers repeatedly. In 1900, a meeting of ratepayers was called as it was urgently necessary to supplement school income. The balance of funds was then £2. Subscriptions were collected from those present, and the chairman, Rev H C Bush, would follow up non-attenders. A subsequent application for funding 'to support funds to meet current expenses' indicates that £34 11s was raised from the ratepayers in 1900, £34 3s in 1901, and £35 12s in 1902. The London and South Western Railway had raised their contribution from three to five guineas in 1902.[11]

Only half of Bishop Burgess' endowment income (stated as £20 p a in December 1880)[12] was initially paid to the new school, which no longer provided education for Milford children. It was only in October 1952, following the conferring of Church of England aided status that a legal adjustment was made to the original Trust to enable the school to be eligible for the full amount.[13]

In 1902, all elementary schools were placed in the hands of a Local Education Authority (LEA). Soon after (1904), the managers at Laverstock needed to provide written contracts for teaching staff – a new practice for the school. LEA directives also covered staffing levels, fire precautions, lavatory provision, and, in 1942, offered two weeks optional school closure to allow children to help with the potato harvest.[14]

In 1911, Managers were advised in a circular from the NS that in single school areas church schools should provide alternative forms of religious teaching. Parents were advised of their right to request this in a notice dated 5 December 1912.[15]

Permission to sell or let the old school building was granted by the Charity Commissioners in 1894. It was finally sold in 1929 having been used for Sunday school, social club and reading room. A personal letter from the buyer, Dr John Benson, gives insight into its state, and some local politics. Dr Benson was then Medical Superintendent of Laverstock Asylum, and a successor to William Finch who made the land available for the first school in 1832. The handwritten letter, addressed to John Hammond, solicitor, reads:

> 'We will buy the old school for £55, not because it is worth anything to us, but because if we do not buy you must sell it to someone else, and we may have all sorts of troubles as to lights and drainage.
> It is a useless shed, but it would probably have value to someone, and you must protect your charity.
> I think we ought to share costs, but as it is a charity, you will probably decide I must bear them all. So be it.
>      J R Benson.
>
> I hope you are keeping very fit, and don't forget – if you want a holiday, that this school house is at your disposal, free of all rents and expenses!'[16]

In 1949, with the school leaving age now 15 years, there was a problem of overcrowding, so senior pupils were moved to secondary schools in Salisbury, the Laverstock school catering for infants and juniors only. By 1964 with housing development in Laverstock, pressure on capacity became acute again, and the school was extended that year (final cost: £22,995). In 1961 and again in 1971, Her Majesty's Inspector, (HMI), reported that, as a short term measure, the LEA was providing taxi transport to St Martin's school for children for whom there were no places in Laverstock. The number on roll (NOR) in April 1976 was 157 and HMI notes a maximum capacity of 160. In July 1976 an angry public meeting was held challenging the highly unpopular restriction of the catchment area to houses north of The Avenue, resulting in some siblings of

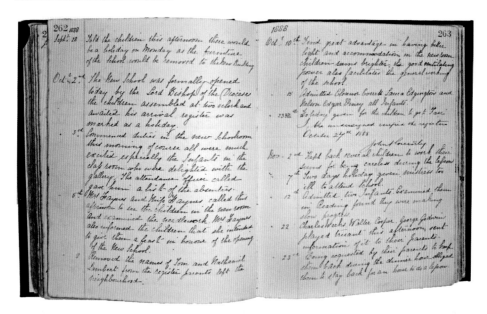

Laverstock CE School Log book 1864-1915, September 1888, pages 262/263 (WSA, F8/500/169/1/1).

existing pupils being denied admission. But by September, such siblings were admitted, and numbers fell thereafter, with NOR 94 recorded for 1981. More families from the newer housing developments were choosing to send their children to St Martin's school.[17]

The school log books from 1864-1976,[18] and especially those covering the period 1864 to 1933 are of great interest, affording a view of local country life and education in that context. They were kept by the headteachers, whose contributions varied greatly in quantity, subject matter, and legibility.

The log books do not provide a complete history of the school. Recording of issues is at times incomplete, with no mention of outcomes. The following notes and quotes are themed and mainly from the log books, but supplemented by notes from the school Managers' minutes 1903-72[19] and official inspections (Diocesan and HMI).[20]

Attendance was monitored closely and log book figures were regularly scrutinised by a manager. Various factors prevented children coming to school. In 1865, three children who had been absent without leave for three months were refused readmission by Rev Greenly (a Trustee). Ten years later, the Diocesan Inspector commented that 'a good many children are left entirely at home, or coming irregularly, who ought to be in constant attendance'. Of children whose fees were paid from parish relief, non-attenders were reported to the Relieving Officer who 'will call on their parents' (1877). Dorothy Ward had been absent for three weeks, and the Attendance Officer, Mr Webb, threatened to issue a summons on her father. Managers' minutes (1914), throw light on the situation, recording that 'Her mother had lost her reason' and 'was in Roundway Hospital, Devizes'. Dorothy's attendance subsequently improved. In 1905 25 children were absent having gone to the Salisbury fair although no holiday had been given.

Between 1865 and 1900 the log book mentions children who should have been in school working in the hay fields and picking potatoes. The 1871 census records show eight under 14s working – six as ploughboys, and two as female servants. By 1891 the census lists ten children as working – ages given as 12 or 13 years, and one girl of 11. Their occupations are stated as: three errand boys, two farm labourers, one brushmaker, one bird scarer, two laundresses. By 1901, only two (both aged 13) worked – as errand boy, and laundress. There was a significant laundry business in Laverstock – probably largely driven by the needs of the asylum, which in the 1891 census declared 42 patients, and in 1901, 48.[21]

Attendance was influenced heavily by weather issues. Some children walked long distances to school. And so, for instance, in 1901 a boy was absent 'for lack of boots'. In 1917, children who walked to school over the downs in the snow arrived with wet feet, and were sent back home. Wet feet in 1933 caused others also to be sent home. In 1923, managers approved 'provision of slippers for children's use in school, with 10s allocated 'for necessitous cases'. In October and November 1870, severe cold required that the children 'were marched ' (to get warm), and resulted both in that year and in 1927, in occasions when written work had to be abandoned. The severe winter weather of early 1947 saw the school closed as the entrance and toilet access were blocked by snow which also drifted into the classroom.

Health problems causing absences of pupils and staff are reported frequently in the log books between 1864 and 1945.

In this period measles, whooping cough, scarlet fever, influenza, diphtheria, consumption (TB), chickenpox and mumps feature often. Measles outbreaks caused school closure in 1873 for one month, and in 1923 for ten days, then a further week. In 1904, over 20 pupils were absent with mumps, 23 with measles in 1911, and in 1892 whooping cough kept over half the infants away. On two occasions the headmistress succumbed – to mumps and whooping cough. The latter resulted in her absence for almost three months in 1915. When there were eight cases of scarlet fever in 1945, the head boy, along with classmates, was admitted to the isolation hospital at Old Sarum, and did not enjoy the experience. It was his last term at school before reaching leaving age, and in effect, he left school some weeks before officially eligible to do so.[22]

The availability of penicillin (1945), and of vaccines for diphtheria in 1942, whooping cough in 1950, with others following later, and comprehensive immunisation programmes, has made the serious disruption of education by infectious disease outbreaks now very rare.

Children were excluded on discovery of ringworm, and lice. A child was excluded in 1929 on grounds of being a danger to others by reason of her 'verminous condition'. Lack of cleanliness led to exclusions too. A child was sent home in 1902, after many previous cautions to his mother, 'his unclean state being offensive to the class.' Chilblains and toothache were each responsible for two recorded absences.

Regular medical inspections (provided for in an Act of 1902) were logged from 1908, school nurse visits from 1924, and dental inspections started in 1917. They often lasted for two to three days, to enable necessary treatment. The headmistress had to act as assistant for an extraction in 1927.

Those most basic necessities, heat, water and sanitation provision often feature in the log books. Heating, initially by coal fires in each of the two schoolrooms, was upgraded by order of the Board of Education in 1928 to boiler and radiators. The boiler was fuelled by coal, and later, coke. In 1917, 'boys were sent out into the lanes to collect loose wood' when coal supply failed. Lack of fuel caused school closure in 1917, 1940 and 1947. Coal fires were used to cover a period of boiler breakdown in 1940. The school was connected to natural gas in 1974. The original school had no water supply, and water had to be brought from nearby dwellings. The new school had pumped well water. Tested for quality in 1917, it was declared 'excellent', but that of 1949 was 'moderately contaminated' and was condemned by the Medical Officer, so children had to cross the road to get water for the school. In January 1950, the HMI report advised insurance cover for this activity. The school was connected to the mains supply in 1959. Sanitation was primitive up until 1961. The original 'privy' system was replaced in 1914 by earth closets with buckets and dry earth, and a sawdust urinal. In 1915, the headteacher requested separate facilities for staff, and managers suggested the coal store could be used. Toilet closet refuse had to be disposed of outside the school perimeter on to neighbouring farm land, by arrangement. In 1924, 'owing to prevalence of Foot and Mouth Disease' resulting temporary alternative arrangements 'gave extra trouble to the caretaker, and so 5/– was voted as a gratuity from the school funds'. Ongoing problems with adequate cleaning and emptying of buckets are recorded up until 1952. In 1961, the LEA required conversion to water closets. In November 1944, Managers' minutes record that electric light was installed. Finance for this had been 'locally raised'.

The original school indenture required reading, writing, and 'cyphering' as the core syllabus, and these subjects were supplemented by a range of others, depending on the interests and skills of the teacher. In 1864, 'subtraction', and the 'manner of making out bills' are mentioned, and pupils 'wrote letters'. In the 1870s the first class were taught weights and measures. Upper standards did reading, and the mistress 'reproved Mary Dicketts for her absurd way of reading and omitting to aspirate h's.' In September 1870, there was 'no writing on paper, the children having taken home their copy books before the holiday. New copy books were given to five children.' In November, the first class began writing in their dictation books, and in March the following year, 'Standard I began writing on paper' rather than slates. In the 1880s the log records 'Drawing lesson. Object lessons were given to the infants on teeth, the cat, leather, the duck' (by the monitress). In the 1900s older boys learned map drawing and drill exercises. Infants tried clay modelling. A knitting lesson was combined with teaching on spiders. In 1916, seven boys were taken to a pruning demonstration locally. Clergy of the parish made frequent visits, and taught Scripture, hymns, catechism, and provided services in church for the pupils during Lent, Easter, and other festivals. Open days for parents in the 1920s gave opportunity for showing pupils' work, as well as dances, songs and recitation. Regular visits to the Salisbury museum for lectures on historical topics are noted, and 'juniors made Plasticine models to illustrate a Bible story'. In the 1930s, eight girls attended cookery lessons in Salisbury. Upper group pupils covered geography, history, nature study (especially local), reading, recitation, composition, arithmetic, drawing, needlework, singing, and folk dancing. The log notes 'further attention needed to speech training'. Road manners, taught by a visiting police sergeant, kindness to animals by the RSPCA, handicrafts by a 'travelling teacher', and swimming for older pupils are noted in the 1940s, when also the top class went to the Southern Railway sportsground for a games session. In the 1970s, lessons on football, netball, French, science, mathematics and woodwork were given by visiting teams of staff and students from several local secondary schools.

Punishments were recorded fairly often, with reasons given, up to the 1940s. In earlier days, calling the monitor by an improper name, idleness, disobedience, neglecting to learn collects, bad language, wilful damage (to the saddle of the mistress's bicycle), climbing on the school roof in the dinner hour, and rudeness to a man working in a neighbouring field, are all cited as punished offences. Caning was often used and mostly, but not exclusively, for boys. In 1928, Jimmy Lake was caned with two others for disobedience and inattention. 'J L smiled on the way back to his seat, so was given an extra stroke'. Parental cooperation in maintaining discipline was not always forthcoming. Parental complaints in 1925, 1926, and 1941 about what was alleged to be excessive punishment had to be officially investigated, but they were not upheld.[23]

The log does not record the start or end of First World War hostilities. Although there are 14 Laverstock men commemorated on the plaque in the parish church, there is no reference to any families of schoolchildren suffering bereavement . War-related entries are sparse, but in 1917 the log records that children collected three dozen eggs in response to a 'national egg collection in July' (for the wounded). In October, Wiltshire children were asked to 'gather blackberries for jam for soldiers and sailors' (too late in the year to be acted on). They also 'gathered five cwt horse chestnuts for munitions purposes'. This was for the home production of acetone used in making cordite for shells. Importing acetone from across the Atlantic was now unreliable, and although it could be made from maize or rice, these were needed for food. Payment of 7s 6d per cwt of chestnuts was made.[24] In 1918, part of the playground was dug up and planted with potatoes.

During the Second World War period, related entries mainly refer to preparation for emergencies, including air raid practice, gas mask practice, inspection and repair of gas masks, and shelter from air raids. A number of raid warnings – ARW – are recorded, but no local bombing. In 1940, after parents had petitioned for an air raid shelter for the school, Brigadier General Kelly visited, and advised that it was unnecessary, and that 'use could be made of the corners of the classroom'. A former pupil remembers 'lots' of ARWs and how pupils were allocated in small groups to different nearby dwellings, to which

1939 page from admission register 1933–70 F8/60/169/1/6/1

they would run. He and a couple of others 'had to go to Mrs. Anderson's house, and huddle under the stairs'. He is not convinced it would have afforded safety.[25]

Eight evacuees from various places were admitted to the school in November 1939. Three returned home within two weeks, two more by the end of the term, and the other three stayed longer (probably until they reached school leaving age).[26] A group of 17 boys evacuated from Lyndhurst School, Portsmouth, came in 1940, swelling the number of children on roll by over 50%. Initially they were accompanied by a teacher, Mr Aherne, who was reported amongst the pupils to have 'a tin leg'.[27] He taught the junior class. The boys' arrival on 1 July is not recorded in the school admission book, and therefore the date of their return home is uncertain. There are no other war-related entries and no record of the start or end of the war.

A number of local people who were active benefactors of the school figure frequently in the log entries. Their support of the school with regard to the wellbeing and education of the children was practical and generous. Their contribution was greatest in the early 1900s. A number served the school as managers or trustees. Rev Greenly 'took all Sunday school regulars to the Wild Beasts Show'. Canon Stanley Baker arranged, and guided, visits to the Cathedral and gave singing lessons, Dr Henry Manning, superintendent of the Laverstock Asylum and a churchwarden, financed visits to the 'panto', to an exhibition of animated photographs, and to Pack's entertainment at the County Hall. He arranged an evening magic lantern show, and conjuring, and his family members gave eatable treats for these occasions. F Hawkins Esq paid for all Day School children to see West's famous cinematograph at County Hall. Various local ladies gave tea parties in the grounds of their homes, or at the school, for children and staff. A number of benefactors gave rewards for good work and attendance.

A number of special occasions were noted in the logs, including a 'treat' in 1931, when children attended a daylight rehearsal of the Tidworth Tattoo. Salisbury's 700th anniversary was marked on 29 and 30 June 1927 by cancellation of afternoon school, and the centenary of St Andrew's Church, Laverstock was celebrated on 8 July 1958 by 'sports, picnic in school grounds, and an impromptu concert by school leavers'.

From the late 19th century the school has been served by a relatively small number of headteachers, with a few staying in post for long periods: **Katherine Shergold** 1876-1914, lived in the centre of the village with her parents. 1891 census records show the family came from Downton, only a few miles away.[28] In 1903, her salary was £90 a year. She was assisted by a number of monitors and teachers. She worked in both old and new schools and her work was commended in the year she retired, when the government inspector's report notes that he was 'particularly pleased with the school as a whole'. **Ethel M Dale** 1918-1947. In 1920, her salary was £208 10s a year. She had a turbulent relationship, at times, with the managers, and some parents. She was a stern disciplinarian, but a head boy from the 1940s describes her as 'Fair. If she gave you a rocket, you knew you deserved it'. He recalled witnessing an incident in the playground, and intervened and fought one of the Portsmouth evacuees, 'Jimmy Corps, who was a bully'. Miss Dale's comment afterwards was 'Well done. He deserved that'.[29] **Miss Belfield** 1950-73. She lived in Ford, and walked to school each day. She made very few log entries. An HMI report comments that she 'talks a great deal and runs a very good school'[30]. **Peter Richardson** 1974-97. His log entries show he was active in encouraging sport, visits to places of interest, short, residential field studies courses, cycling proficiency instruction, and school clubs, with elected pupil officers. The school is currently enjoying stable leadership under his successor, the present head, **Mrs Karen Walker**, who is responsible for the education of 195 pupils on roll (December 2016).

Various other, miscellaneous matters were judged worthy of mention. For instance, in 1898, during a severe thunderstorm, 'all work was suspended for one hour and children were told not to touch pens and needles to reduce risk of lightning strike'.

Several girls who lived in Ford and walked to school, arrived 'very late' in 1907, and consequently 'lost their mark' and 'were sent home to learn a lesson'.

Three families were 'compelled to live in the town' in 1904, as they had no accommodation, their dwellings having 'been condemned'. In 1908, the Beach family, with a poor attendance record moved 'at the Michaelmas changing of hands' (quarter day). (One of the boys in this family, aged 12 years, was only at the standard of a first year junior class pupil.) Fourteen children left for the same reason in 1910, and nine more in 1913. In 1912, two 'caravan children staying a few months in the neighbourhood' were admitted.

In 1909, Frank England, congenitally deaf and one of three siblings, was living in Laverstock with an aunt, after the death of his mother. The LEA proposed he be educated at a special school in Exeter. The 1893 Education Act provided for special education of such children. His aunt refused to release him. She later agreed when a younger sibling (who was living in Hampshire) was sent with him.

Between 1904 and 1917, eight 13 year-old boys were officially permitted to leave school for agricultural work before reaching the normal school leaving age.

In the winter of 1923, cocoa was provided for children. In 1935, 'milk was given to all children who paid halfpenny a bottle, and will continue'. Hot dinners were first provided in 1944 (prepared elsewhere and transported in). Food was not cooked on the premises until May 1965, after a kitchen had been built.

In 1950, the school fence needed attention, evidenced by the presence of cattle in the school grounds. Cattle had also entered the grounds in 1948 and damaged the school garden.

The managers, headmistress, Parish Council, and school inspectors had long been concerned for the safety of children on the narrow road, without pavements, outside the school. Road safety was taught in school. From 1963 up to 1966, repeated attempts to recruit a school crossing warden were made, with no responses to the advertisements. In 1966, in a shadow of things to come, Miss Belfield, headmistress, made managers aware that 'a hazard was being caused by the cars of parents collecting their children at the school entrance and obstructing the children's view of the traffic'.

Thus the log books have afforded a varied, sometimes amusing and colourful picture of both this village school, and the rural community and way of life which has been its setting. The school remains a central part of Laverstock life, reflecting as it has done over the past 180 years, many aspects of its community's culture.

## Sources

*Documents held at Wiltshire and Swindon Archive, Chippenham (WSA)*
Diocese of Salisbury Land for National School 1832-93. D/632/2/10
Laverstock CE School log books from 1864-1976 F8/500/169/1/1,2,3
Postcards and Photos 1324/56
WCC Admissions register 1933-70  F8/600/169/1/6/1
WCC Draft deeds and papers  1887-1947 F8/600/169/1/1/2
WCC General Education Committee Cuttings books 1905-39, 1940-62.  F8/230/2/1,3.
WCC HMI reports  1920-93  F8/300/176
WCC lease of land for school 1887  F8/600/169/1/1/1
WCC Managers' minutes 1903-1972 F8/600/169/1/3/1,2
WCC Minutes of Bishop Burgess Trustees and accounts 1931-61   F8/600/169/1/4/1
WCC Primary school correspondence 1901-1928, 1961-70  F8/600/169/1/26/2
WCC Primary school Diocesan inspection book 1874-89 F8/600/169/1/12/1
WCC Primary school plans 1884-1961 F8/600/169/1/22/1
*Documents held in National Archive under ' St Andrew's Primary school'.*
Bishop Burgess Educational Foundation 1880-1931 ED 49/8205
Ministry of Education, Laverstock National School files 1872-1912 ED 21/18460
*Other Sources.*
Gillard D (2011) *Education in England: A brief history.*
National Censuses 1851-1911
Reminiscences given verbally by Mr P Annetts to S A Evans on 3 January 2017
School log book September 1976-2001 (kept in school. December 2016)
www.historyextra.com/conker (Dec 2016)


## Notes

1   Diocese of Salisbury Land for National School 1832-93  D/632/2/10
2   Laverstock CE School log book from 1864-1915 F8/500/169/1/1
3   WCC Primary school Diocesan inspection book 1874-89 F8/600/169/1/12/1
4   Laverstock CE School log book from 1864-1915 F8/500/169/1/1
5   Ministry of Education, Laverstock National School files  1872-1912 ED 21/18460
6   WCC lease of land for school 1887  F8/600/169/1/1/1; Diocese of Salisbury Land for National School 1832-93  D/632/2/10. [The NS was founded in 1811 and aimed to establish a church school in every parish and promote the education of the poor in the principles of the Established Church. There were 12,000 affiliated schools in 1851.]
7   Diocese of Salisbury Land for National School 1832-93  D/632/2/10
8   Laverstock CE School log book from 1864-1915 F8/500/169/1/1
9   WCC Primary school correspondence  1901-1928 F8/600/169/1/26/2
10  Diocese of Salisbury Land for National School  1832-93 D/632/2/10
11  WCC Primary school correspondence  1901-1928 F8/600/169/1/26/2; Laverstock CE School log book from 1864-1915 F8/500/169/1/1
12  Bishop Burgess Educational Foundation 1880-1931 ED 49/8205
13  WCC Primary  school correspondence 1961-70  F8/600/169/1/26/2
14  WCC Managers' minutes 1903-1972 F8/600/169/1/3/1,2
15  WCC Primary school correspondence  1901-1928, 1961-70  F8/600/169/1/26/2
16  WCC Draft deeds and papers  1887-1947 F8/600/169/1/1/2

17  WCC HMI reports 1920-93  F8/300/176; Laverstock CE School log book from 1933-1976  F8/500/169/1/3; School log book September 1976-2001 (kept in school December 2016)

18  Laverstock CE School log books from 1864-1976  F8/500/169/1/1,2,3; School log book September 1976-2001 (kept in school Dec. 2016)

19  WCC Managers' minutes 1903-1972  F8/600/169/1/3/1,2

20  WCC Primary school Diocesan inspection book 1874-89 F8/600/169/1/12/1; WCC HMI reports 1920-56  F8/300/155

21  National Census 1871 Public Record Office ref: RG 10 1952; National Census 1891 Public Record Office ref: RG 12 1618; National Census 1901 Public Record Office ref: RG 13 1951

22  Reminiscences given verbally by  Mr P Annetts to S A Evans on 3 January 2017

23  WCC Managers' minutes 1903-1972 F8/600/169/1/3/1,2

24  www.historyextra.com/conker (January 2017)

25  Reminiscences given verbally by  Mr P Annetts to S A Evans on 3 January 2017

26  WCC Admissions register 1933-70  F8/600/169/1/6/1

27  Reminiscences given verbally by  Mr P Annetts to S A Evans on 3 January 2017

28  National Census 1891 Public Record Office ref: RG 12 1618

29  Reminiscences given verbally by  Mr P Annetts to S A Evans on 3 January 2017

30  WCC HMI reports 1920-93 F8/300/176

Salisbury Cathedral Library: interior from North end

# 'Not Undeserving of Notice': Salisbury Cathedral Library through nine centuries

## Peter Hoare

Hidden away above the east cloister, up a thirteenth-century spiral staircase from the south transept, Salisbury Cathedral Library is a visual delight. Within this late-medieval room modern bookcases in seventeenth-century style contain ten thousand books large and small. The printed books range from the fifteenth to the twenty-first centuries, and the earliest of the 225 manuscripts dates back to the ninth century, well before the present Cathedral or even its predecessor

at Old Sarum. Theology dominates, as it has from the beginning. The Use of Sarum, the liturgy which spread from Salisbury across much of England in the Middle Ages and was the inspiration of the Book of Common Prayer, is well represented, from manuscripts and early printed versions to modern interpretations. The Reformation and early continental printing are prominent, but there is much else: seventeenth-century science in abundance, the classics from scholarly editions to schoolboy texts, English history and literature, and music from medieval times to recent decades, reflecting Salisbury's rich choral and liturgical heritage.

Salisbury Cathedral Library above the East Cloister

The Library began in the 1080s, soon after the first cathedral was built at Old Sarum, when Bishop Osmund set up a scriptorium producing books for the 'scribes and scholars' attracted to the new establishment.[1] About sixty of the manuscripts written at Old Sarum remain in the Cathedral Library today – the largest collection of Norman manuscripts in England still in the hands of their original owner. These were mostly biblical studies and patristics (the works of the early Church Fathers like St Augustine and St Jerome), quite distinctive to look at – written for use, not for display, often on poor quality vellum, unlike the splendid illuminations found elsewhere.

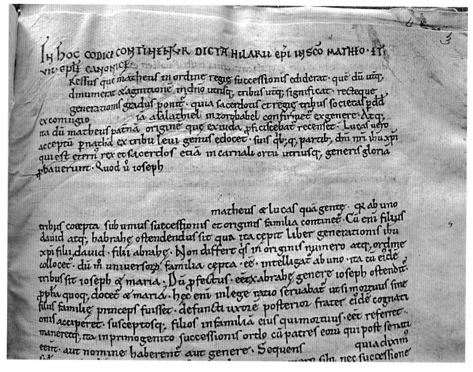

Opening page of Bishop Hilary of Poitiers on St Matthew's Gospel, one of the many manuscripts written at Old Sarum in the early 12th century (Salisbury MS 124). By kind permission of the Dean & Chapter of Salisbury Cathedral

Osmund can be considered the true founder of today's Cathedral Library, though he had died 120 years before work began on the present Cathedral in 'New Sarum'. The library he helped to create at Old Sarum was moved to the new location by the mid-thirteenth century and forms a precious core for today's Library. The manuscripts may have been kept with the archives in the muniment room off the south-east transept (now the choir practice room) and probably in chests like the one now in the north choir aisle. The original Old Sarum books were joined by more manuscripts, older and younger, many acquired from elsewhere rather than written in Salisbury - but mostly still theological texts in Latin. Donations and bequests were the main source and can be traced from inscriptions in the books: Dean Walter Scammell gave a fine lectionary as early as 1277, specifically for the use of the canons of the Cathedral, and with a note at the end of the volume threatening Anathema on anyone who should remove it, and in 1327 Chancellor Henry de la Wyle left the Cathedral fifteen volumes, of which eight survive in the Library.[2]

About 1445 the Library received a 13th-century copy of Petrus Comestor's *Historia Scholastica*, ostensibly from Richard Praty, bishop of Chichester - a Biblical paraphrase on the curriculum of universities across Europe. The manuscript has an inscription 'It is a lie that this book belonged to Richard Praty - he had had it from the Chapter of Salisbury when he was Chancellor there', so it really belonged here all the time. In 1447 Archdeacon John Stopyndon bequeathed four books to Salisbury, two of them still here, and Canon Thomas Cyrceter, who died in 1452, left the Library at least 13 manuscripts still extant, mostly sermons and other theological works but including another copy of Comestor and Chaucer's English translation of Boethius.

Two of Cyrceter's manuscripts say they are 'to be chained in the new library *(cathenandus in libraria nova)*'. This refers to the momentous decision by the Dean and Chapter in January 1445 to create a library.[3] This was a major undertaking: a building extending over the full length of the east range of the cloister, as seen in seventeenth-century engravings of the Cathedral. It was built with stone

Detail of John Collins's South-West Prospect of the Cathedral (after Nicholas Yeates), c1671, showing the full length of the Library above the Cloister before the reduction in size made in 1758. By kind permission of Salisbury Museum.

from a quarry owned by the convent of Shaftesbury, in exchange for a cope for the abbess given in 1446; and King Henry VI gave oak from the Royal forests to fit it out. The southern half of the new building was intended for the Library, while the northern end was a lecture-room used by the Chancellor. The Library must have resembled Duke Humfrey's Library at Oxford (now at the heart of the Bodleian Library), built at much the same time. Salisbury's Dean Gilbert Kymer was also Chancellor of Oxford University and knew Duke Humfrey well: he must have been closely concerned in both library buildings. Duke Humfrey's had lecterns and benches between the windows, and the layout at Salisbury must have been similar.[4] Such lecterns, with books on the sloping surface or flat on a shelf below, were the standard way of storing books, with books often chained to the lectern for security. (The Library today contains a collection of chains, but we do not know which books they came from: some will have been on manuscripts, but many printed books still show signs of having been chained, even well into the eighteenth century.)

Barely a hundred years after the new library was built, the Reformation affected both the Cathedral and its Library. Monastic libraries throughout England were scattered after the Dissolution, when at Malmesbury Abbey, for example, 'the manuscripts flew about like butterflies'.[5] The Cathedral however was not monastic, and escaped with much of its Library collections intact. More than 200 of its medieval manuscripts have survived, most at Salisbury itself but some elsewhere.[6] Under King Edward VI all the old Latin service books were ordered to be destroyed from Christmas Day 1549,[7] and under Queen Elizabeth I there were bonfires of 'papist' service books in the Close, to which the churches of St Thomas and St Edmund contributed – but some breviaries, graduals and psalters have survived. In 1573, a hundred-year-old manuscript Processional was annotated by the Dean and Canons, who had 'found therein many superstitious things, contrary to the word of God and the laws of this kingdom, which by unanimous consent they ordered to be abrogated'.[8] Like some other manuscripts the Processional has indeed had sections deleted or cut away – but it was not destroyed and is still in the Library.

Following the depredations to monastic libraries, Archbishop Matthew Parker set out to preserve Anglo-Saxon and other early manuscripts, partly to provide ammunition for the new Church of England settlement. (Salisbury may not have been very promising: John Leland, who travelled through England and Wales for Henry VIII in 1534-43, had mentioned a mere six books there, only one of them still with us.)[9] In January 1569 Bishop John Jewel responded to Parker's request:

accordinge to my promisse I have ransacked our poore Librarie of Sarisburie and have founde nothing worthy the findinge, savinge onely one booke written in the Saxon tongue, whiche I minde to sende to your Grace by the nexte conveniente messinger.

Jewel missed one of the Library's great treasures, the fine tenth-century Gallican Psalter with an Anglo-Saxon translation between the lines of the Latin text. The manuscript he did send to Parker, King Alfred's translation of St Gregory, is now at Cambridge.[10] Jewel's reference to 'our poore librarie' reflects Leland's survey, and his successor Edmund Geste called it 'now decayed'

Late 10th-century Psalter in the Gallican version, showing an initial D and the interlinear translation into Anglo-Saxon (Salisbury MS 150). By kind permission of the Dean & Chapter of Salisbury Cathedral

less than ten years later. There was a later tradition, not substantiated, that Jewel had set up a library: an inscription said to have been on the wall (and copied in 1578 into a book still in the Library) said that 'this library (*bibliotheca*) was built (*exstructa*) by Jewel' but supplied with books (*instructa vero libris*) by Geste; perhaps Jewel gave a bookcase rather than a whole library that has now disappeared.[11]

With Bishop Edmund Geste the Library began to take its present form. When he came to Salisbury in 1571 the 'poore library' consisted largely if not entirely of manuscripts. Six years later Geste left his whole collection of printed books to the Library, hugely increasing its size. His will bequeathed 'to the Library of the Cathedral Church of Sar[um] now decayed all my Books'.[12] His memorial brass in the Morning Chapel shows him with a book in his hand, and records that 'he left a great store of the best books such as scarcely any library can match, to be kept in this church for studious persons to use in perpetuity'.

The Library has 1204 printed works surviving from Geste's collection, in 684 volumes (with a further 116 works less certainly his), in a fine collection of contemporary bindings. This is one of England's largest contemporary accumulations of Reformation theology - especially books printed on the Continent.[13] The scholarly bishop clearly used his books heavily (his appalling handwriting helps to identify his books): his library was strong in liturgical works, which he used in working on revisions to the *Book of Common Prayer.* Religious controversy, both Protestant and Catholic, features strongly: more than 30 works by Martin Luther survive among Geste's books, and much by his colleagues and opponents. Rare editions are common, and his bequest is a major element in the Library's holdings of early printing - nearly half of the Library's forty incunabula (books printed before 1501) came from him - and altogether it is one of the principal jewels in the Library's crown.

One of Geste's books illustrates the multifarious attractions of early books. His copy of Balbus's *Catholicon,* a medieval dictionary of the Bible, was printed at Venice in 1497 (only three other copies of this edition are recorded in the UK). Soon after being bound it was used by someone with very non-ecclesiastical interests: the flyleaf records the steps for twenty French *basses danses,* rare evidence for late-medieval courtly dances.[14] The dance steps are partly overwritten by memoranda in Geste's almost illegible hand. Also, the binder had used some waste pages from Caxton's 1483 edition of Gower's *Confessio Amantis,* which were recognised and extracted only in the twentieth century - the Library's only example of Caxton's printing (though we have his translation of the *Golden Legend,* printed by his pupil Wynkyn de Worde about 1493).

A selection of Bishop Geste's books, showing shelf-numbers (B33 etc.) on the fore-edges. By kind permission of the Dean & Chapter of Salisbury Cathedral

Unfortunately Geste's collection is not now all shelved together. When his books arrived, new shelving must have been needed: judging from the shelf-marks still visible on the fore-edges of many of his books, they were kept on shelves (not lecterns), in broad subject groups.[15] This arrangement may have lasted until the re-building of the library in 1758; a visitor in the early eighteenth century noted that 'The library is fitted up with seats and cases for books in a very ancient but ordinary manner', perhaps still in the sixteenth-century layout.[16]

So the library went forward into the seventeenth century with strong printed and manuscript collections, though it is less clear how much scholarly activity was going on in the Cathedral. There were certainly scholars among the bishops and deans, some of whom left books to the library; others preferred bequests to their Oxford or Cambridge colleges. Dean John Gordon left all his books to the Cathedral Library in 1619, but most of them seem to have gone to his executor instead.[17]

In 1622 Patrick Young, librarian to King James VI and I, surveyed several cathedral libraries. His Salisbury catalogue lists 181 books - but omits thirty or more of the Library's medieval manuscripts. Several manuscripts listed by Young have now disappeared, many for reasons unknown – and at least four manuscripts from Salisbury ended up in the Royal Library, no doubt at Young's request.[18] A few years later Thomas James, Bodley's Librarian at Oxford, borrowed six manuscripts from Salisbury, all important early Patristic texts: these books are still in the Bodleian, all marked 'Liber Bibliothecæ Saresburiensis'.

More manuscripts left Salisbury in 1640 but some were finally returned. Dean Richard Baylie lent five books to James Ussher, archbishop of Armagh, for his own scholarly purposes. Two of them were plundered from Ussher's house in Chelsea in 1643: one of these ended up in Trinity College Dublin, and the other disappeared entirely. In 1650 three of these manuscripts, all from the Old Sarum library, were formally returned to Dean Baylie (by then also President of St John's College, Oxford), but he left them in the hands of Bodley's Librarian 'until the Deane and the chapter shall call for them'. Perhaps the times were not propitious for sending books across England. The Bodleian agreed to return them in 1679, but asked to keep them 'for some time' for the use of Dr John Fell, Bishop of Oxford – and after Fell's death in 1686 they returned not to Salisbury but to the Bodleian. Eventually, in 1985, thanks to a paper-trail of official correspondence, Salisbury persuaded Oxford to send them back, along with a fine Sarum breviary from Great Bedwyn that had reached the Bodleian from a bequest of Bishop Goodman of Gloucester. These are now our MSS. 221-224, back with their companions after an absence of 345 years.[19] It can be dangerous to allow books out of the Library!

During the Civil War and under the Commonwealth there was more than a degree of confusion – not surprisingly since deans and chapters had been abolished in 1648 by government decree – and documentary evidence is poor. In 1653 Dutch prisoners confined in the cloisters broke windows there and in the Library, but no more damage was done to the building. The books in the Library were apparently 'embezzled in the times of the troubles except those which are left and of little value', according to a response to Seth Ward's episcopal visitation of 1672.[20] Nonetheless, Salisbury, unlike Wells and some other cathedrals, preserved much of its Library through to the Restoration, when collections began to grow again. Bishop Henchman acquired Salisbury's copy of the 'Sealed Book' of the 1662 *Book of Common Prayer,* with its Royal letters patent, for which he requested reimbursement from the Dean and Chapter – the book is still in the Library though it has lost its Great Seal.[21] After Dean Baylie's death his son gave the Cathedral £40 to buy books in his memory: a handsome armorial bookplate dated 1668 records the gift.[22] In the 1680s more additions came in, making extra book-shelves necessary, from gifts by Chancellor Richard Drake and Prebendary Dr Richard Watson.[23]

The next major bequest came from Bishop Seth Ward, who died in 1689 after 22 years as bishop, when he did much to revive the fortunes of his cathedral and diocese. Ward had been Professor of Astronomy at Oxford and one of the founding members of the Royal Society; he persuaded his friend Christopher Wren to survey the Cathedral structure in 1668, and Wren's report is still in the Cathedral Archives. Ward left half of his collection to the Library and half to his nephews: his bequest was remarkably wide-ranging. Over 450 of his books have been identified in the Library: they include some theology, as one would expect, but also much science, particularly astronomy, mathematics and anatomy, with many books inscribed to him by the authors. This is not unexpected, given his background, but it gives the Cathedral Library an unusually scientific flavour.[24] As with Edmund Geste's books, most of Seth Ward's are in their original bindings.

The Library's collections continued to grow through the earlier eighteenth century. The subject coverage became wider - though theology still dominated - and more books were in English. Canon Isaac Walton, who died in 1719, left £150 to appoint a Librarian, and his own considerable collection of books and pamphlets also came to the Library: they included, notably, twenty-seven books signed by his father, the famous writer Izaak Walton, though sadly not *The Compleat Angler*.[25] Remarkably, many of the Walton books have marks of having been chained, though the actual clasps are no longer there: this must have been done after the books came to the Library, though 1719 is late for books to be chained. A later descendant of the Walton family, Herbert Hawes, rector of St Edmund's (d. 1837) left to the Library 'an extensive collection of books in the learned languages and a valuable series of works of Divinity', including some signed by Izaak Walton (more of Izaak's books have been acquired more recently).[26]

Another dramatic building project occurred three hundred years after the 'new' library and lecture-room had been built. In November 1758 the Chapter ordered the demolition of the southern end of the range over the east cloister, which had been found 'much too heavy to be properly supported'. The lecture-room, at the northern end, had its roof replaced by a lighter construction, and the Library moved into its space, 'fitted up in a neat and convenient manner for the reception of the present books'.[27] The Library had reached its present shape, 66 feet long and occupying five of the original ten bays, and still reached only by the spiral staircase from the south transept. There is little evidence of what the 'neat and convenient manner' actually was: a catalogue of 1815 assigns books to 'compartments' rather than presses or book-cases, but that does not correspond to today's arrangement.

Despite its new accommodation, it seems that the Library was once again neglected. The antiquary Sir Thomas Phillipps, who lived in the Close in the 1820s, reported broken windows in the Library and jackdaws perching on Anglo-Saxon manuscripts lying 'unregarded' on tables and floor. Beriah Botfield, writing on English cathedral libraries in 1849, reported that Salisbury's books had 'suffered severely from neglect', not least because of 'the long interval during which this ancient Cathedral was suffered to remain in the most neglected state'. Nonetheless he gives a good account of the Library's collections, judging that 'when the cobwebs of the last century have been brushed away, some works may probably be found not undeserving of notice'.[28] Nineteenth-century donations do show positive growth, and by 1880 the Library was increased by over a thousand volumes from the bequest

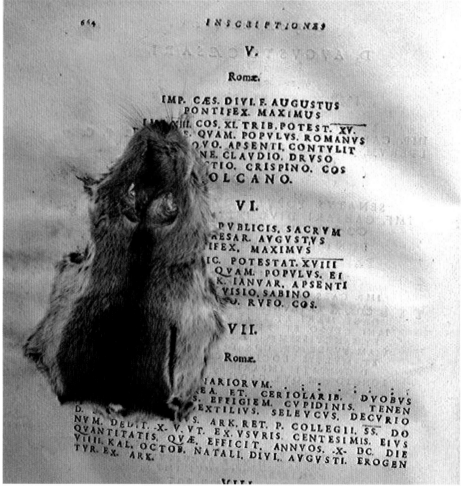

Suetonius's works (Paris, 1684), showing the squashed mouse killed by choirboys in the late 18th century. By kind permission of the Dean & Chapter of Salisbury Cathedral

of Dean Henry Parr Hamilton - including some science as well as theology and history. More new shelving was added at the south end of the library to accommodate Hamilton's books, making the room more congested.

Dean Hamilton's collection arrived just as the Library's first printed catalogue, by Rev. Storer Marshall Lakin, was nearing publication: it was recorded in a 25-page supplement to the main catalogue.[29] Lakin's 300-page catalogue is a considerable achievement, and is still in use, though some books listed in it are now missing. The shelf-marking system printed in it, perhaps devised about the same time, has remained in use ever since. The Cathedral wisely brought in Edward Maunde Thompson (later Sir Edward, and director of the British Museum) to catalogue the manuscripts, and his entries remain valuable.[30]

A period of greater interest in the library followed the new catalogue. The next large collection arrived in 1899, from the heirs of Canon Thomas Luck Kingsbury - a huge accumulation rich in Reformation literature, German history, Jewish culture (with several liturgical books in Hebrew) and much more. Some of the Kingsbury material has not yet been catalogued and cannot be properly evaluated, but again it seems to have required more shelving to be erected, this time at the north end, high up above the wall-shelving largely filled with Seth Ward's books, and literally affronting the corbel head of Henry VI above the Library door. A series of scholarly librarians included Chancellor Christopher Wordsworth, brother of Bishop John Wordsworth, and many books were presented by him. Bishop Wordsworth himself died in 1911, and many of his books, especially on liturgy, were transferred from the Bishop's Palace. The Bishop's distinctive purple ink-stamp is found in books all over the library, so these too were not kept together, again making them harder to assess.

Fifty-odd books from the library of the Choristers' School were deposited in the Cathedral Library in 1918, with an attractive bookplate dated 1866, though its history goes back much further.[31] The books, many showing signs of heavy schoolboy use, are predominantly classical texts, and several have donation inscriptions from former students from around 1700. Two books, a 1553 Cicero and a 1684 Suetonius, also show dramatic evidence of the choirboys' leisure pursuits, with the grisly remains of mice trapped between the pages.

By the start of the Second World War in 1939 the Library was crowded, with glass display cases at the north end, where notable items from the Library and archives - including Magna Carta - were regularly on show to the visiting public.[32] This practice was suspended during the War, when the manuscripts and muniments, together with some printed books, were 'evacuated' to safer depositories such as a quarry near Bradford-on-Avon under Government control. Unfortunately many suffered from damp and needed drastic repair on their return. This explains why most of the manuscripts no longer have their medieval bindings; many were rebound by Harry Bailey, a Salisbury bookbinder who acted as assistant librarian and wrote about the history of the library and its bindings.[33]

For forty years of the twentieth century Dr Elsie Smith (1890-1977) served as assistant librarian or librarian. She was particularly devoted to Magna Carta (it may not be true that she stored it under her bed for safety, but she did have a massive safe installed in the Library to house it securely). She also oversaw the refurbishment in 1952-53, when the whole Library was cleaned and the shelving re-arranged. The display cases remained in position, with the manuscripts stored beneath them, and income from visitors allowed the Library to buy back some lost manuscripts.

In retrospect it is clear that having the Library on the 'tourist route' could not be sustained, in view of losses to books and general conservation considerations, and in 1978-1980 the Library underwent major restoration. The medieval floorboards were cleaned and made draught-proof; the old book-cases were replaced by handsome ones on seventeenth-century lines, made using elm from trees from the Close felled during the Dutch elm disease epidemic. The design fits the medieval room very well and has allowed extra shelves to be fitted in. The manuscripts now have their own securely-locked cupboard, and the display cases have gone, allowing more space for readers. The huge task of cleaning and shelving all the books in their proper sequences before the re-opening in 1983 fell to Suzanne Eward, who took over as Librarian in 1980, though she had been working in the Library for several years, cataloguing the pre-1701 books and reporting them to union catalogues. She also catalogued most of the Library afresh - all the early books and most of the later ones - in a new card catalogue, using modern bibliographical tools essential for the proper identification of books, and made many contacts with scholars world-wide. All this has helped to reveal the Library's treasures to a wider scholarly audience.

One other collection has come to the Library relatively recently. The parish library from Gillingham in Dorset was deposited in 1994: a collection of c. 270 volumes of theology, almost all printed in English before 1732, and most with a bookplate of 1735 recording their gift by the Freke family.[34] It is good that the Cathedral Library is able to offer hospitality to such collections, complementing its own holdings.

At the same time as the reconstruction, changes in access to the Library were introduced, to discourage casual visitors, though the Library remained available to scholars as it always had been. This led to its being somewhat lost to sight to many in the Cathedral, and in recent years a more relaxed policy has been introduced. Following Suzanne Eward's retirement as Archivist and Librarian, Chancellor Edward Probert won support for the Library and Archives from the Heritage Lottery Fund and the Sackler Foundation. Latterly a more open policy for the Library has made the collections more accessible to visitors as well as to the scholarly world, and Suzanne Eward's successor Emily Naish has introduced public talks and regular visits (closely supervised), not least as part of the Cathedral's educational outreach programme. An open-access reference collection of books on the history of the Cathedral has been created, and an on-line catalogue is planned. The Cathedral's web-site regularly includes blog posts and announcements of library events, and the Library is once more coming to be more widely appreciated as one of the Cathedral's great treasures. As Beriah Botfield wrote in 1849, cobwebs have been swept away and it is now recognised to be indeed 'not undeserving of notice'.

## Notes

1  Webber, Teresa, 1992, *Scribes and Scholars at Salisbury Cathedral c. 1075-c.1125,* Oxford University Press; Ker, N R, 1976, 'The beginnings of Salisbury Cathedral Library', in Alexander, J J G and Gibson, M T (ed) *Medieval Learning and Literature: essays presented to R W Hunt,* Clarendon Press; reprinted in Ker, N R *Books, Collectors and Libraries: studies in the medieval heritage,* ed A G Watson, Hambledon Press 1985, 143-173.

2  Stroud, Daphne, 2001, 'Salisbury Cathedral Library: bequest of Henry de la Wyle, Chancellor 1313-1329', unpublished typescript in the Cathedral Library.

3  Salisbury Cathedral Archives, Chapter Act Book 10, 'Hutchins', 83; Clark 1902, 115; Tatton-Brown, Tim, & Crook, John, 2009, *Salisbury Cathedral: the making of a medieval masterpiece,* Salisbury Cathedral, 102.

4  Gillam, Stanley, 1988, *The Divinity School and Duke Humfrey's Library at Oxford,* Clarendon Press, 11-13 and plates 9-10.

5  Aubrey, John, 1992, *Brief Lives: a modern English version,* ed by Richard Barber, Boydell Press, 15.

6  Lakin, S M, 1880, *A Catalogue of the Library of the Cathedral Church of Salisbury,* Spottiswoode & Co, v; Ker, N R, 1964, *Medieval Libraries of Great Britain: a list of surviving books.* Second edition, Royal Historical Society, 171-176; and *Supplement to the second edition,* ed A G Watson, Royal Historical Society, 1987, 60-61.

7  Brown, Sarah, 1999, *Sumptuous and Richly Adorn'd : the decoration of Salisbury Cathedral,* Stationery Office, 33.

8  Lack, Alastair, 2014, *Processions and Other Late Mediaeval Ceremonies of Salisbury Cathedral: a facsimile of Salisbury Cathedral MS148.* Second edition, the author, fol. 44b.

9  Toulmin Smith, Lucy (ed ), 1907, *The Itinerary of John Leland,* Bell, vol 1, 263.

10  Ker, N R, 1949, 'Salisbury Cathedral manuscripts and Patrick Young's catalogue', *Wiltshire Magazine,* 53, 153-83; reprinted with further notes by A G Watson in Ker, N R 1985, *Books, Collectors and Libraries: studies in the medieval heritage,* ed A G Watson, Hambledon Press, 175-208.

11  Ker, N R, 1977, 'The Library of John Jewel', *Bodleian Library Record* 9(5), 256-65.

12  Dugdale, Henry Geast, 1840, *The Life and Character of Edmund Geste,* Pickering, 55-56.

13 Selwyn, David, 2017, *Edmund Geste and his Books: reconstructing the library of a Cambridge don and Elizabethan bishop,* Bibliographical Society.

14 Wilson, David, 2012, *The Basse Dance Handbook: text and context,* Pendragon Press, 113-122.

15 Selwyn 2017, Appendix V, 347-73.

16 Eward, Suzanne, 1983, *Salisbury Cathedral Library,* Salisbury Cathedral Library, 6.

17 Weller, Ralph B, 1997, *The Strange Case of John Gordon (1544-1619), double-agent and Dean of Salisbury,* the author, 43-44.

18 Ker 1949; Webber, Teresa, 1990, 'Patrick Young, Salisbury Cathedral Manuscripts and the Royal Collection', *English Manuscript Studies,* 2, 283-90

19 Ker, N R and Piper, A J, 1992, *Medieval Manuscripts in British Libraries,* vol 4, Paisley-York, Clarendon Press, 253-266.

20 Selwyn 2017, Introduction, 57, footnote 53.

21 Eward, Suzanne, 2009, '17th-century life and strife at Salisbury Cathedral: lecture given at the 750th anniversary conference', *Spire,* 22-31, 26.

22 Lee, Brian North, 2004, *Some Church of England Parochial Library and Cathedral Ex-Libris,* Bookplate Society, 120-121.

23 Eward 1983, 4.

24 Fletcher, J M J, 1939, 'Seth Ward, bishop of Salisbury, 1667-1689', *WANHM,* 49, 1-16; an offprint is in the Library.

25 Bevan, Jonquil, 1980, 'Some books from Izaak Walton's library', *The Library,* 6th series 2, 259-63; Bevan, Jonquil, 1985, *Izaak Walton and Salisbury Cathedral Library,* Salisbury Cathedral.

26 *The Gentleman's Magazine* 1837, vol 7, 549.

27 Salisbury Cathedral Archives, Chapter Act Book CH/1/21; Clark, J W, 1902, *The Care of Books: an essay on the development of libraries and their fittings, from the earliest times to the end of the eighteenth century,* Cambridge University Press, 115.

28 Botfield, Beriah, 1849, *Notes on the Cathedral Libraries of England,* Pickering, 405-416.

29 Lakin 1880, 273-298.

30 Lakin 1880, 1-44.

31 Lee 2004, 122-123.

32 Bailey, Harry, 1978, *Salisbury Cathedral Library: a brief account of its history and contents,* Friends of Salisbury Cathedral, 14.

33 Bailey, Harry, 1950?, *Short Notes on the Bookbindings of Salisbury Cathedral Library,* Salisbury Cathedral Library; Bailey 1978.

34 Perkin, Michael, 2004, *A Directory of the Parochial Libraries of the Church of England and the Church in Wales;* first ed by Neil Ker, revised edition by Michael Perkin, Bibliographical Society, 215-216; Lee 2004, 54.

**Note**: All photography by Emily Naish

# Bemerton St John
# A Building Reborn

## Peter Webster

### Background

In 1977 the Victoria and Albert Museum staged an exhibition entitled *Change and Decay: the future of our churches.* Its director at the time was Sir Roy Strong. In a lecture thirty years later he bemoaned the fact that the exhibition had had so little impact; the plight of parish churches was still largely overlooked by politicians, and indeed by almost the entire populace.   The transcript of his lecture[1] is worth reading. It sums up admirably how church buildings are so lightly regarded and stresses their value as community assets.

The Church of Bemerton St John the Evangelist (St John's) typified the situation described by Strong. The Grade II★ listed building[2] was built in what is now Lower Bemerton in the early 1860s to cater for the expansion of the local population resulting from the coming of the railways to Salisbury. It was designed by T H Wyatt, one of the foremost church architects of the time, and dedicated to the memory of Bemerton's poet-priest George Herbert (1593-1633).[3] Like most churches, its regular congregation had seen a steady decline in the second half of the twentieth century. The situation was exacerbated by the creation of the Bemerton Heath housing estate following the Second World War, which had the effect of displacing the centre of gravity of Bemerton Parish to the north of the Wilton Road and resulted in the building of Bemerton St Michael in 1957 to serve this new community.

By the turn of the millennium, the number of regular Sunday service attendees at St John's had fallen to a couple of dozen, on whom the costs of maintaining the building fell. The situation reached crisis point in 2007 when it became clear that the church's heating system, which had been in terminal decline for some years, finally expired. The estimated cost of replacement was £45,000. The Parochial Church Council (PCC) took a decision[4] that such expenditure could not be justified for a building used one day a week by so few people, and declared the church closed for regular worship. Thereafter it would be used only for special services, weddings and funerals. Its longer term future remained unresolved.

## Project Inception

Not unnaturally, the residents of Lower Bemerton were concerned at this turn of events and there was much discussion about the future of such a prominent building. The Rector took the view that any proposals for its future had to come from those living nearby; if there was a will to preserve the building, it would be for them to find a way of doing so. Some residents were aware of Sir Roy Strong's recent intervention, and his view that 'So much concerning the problem of churches could be solved by giving the building back to the community as its meeting place with adequate safeguards for worship'.[5]  In March 2008 they agreed to test this by distributing a leaflet inviting local residents to a public meeting in order to explain the position and establish the level of support for preserving the building.

The meeting was well attended, and there was general agreement that the community should try to find a way of making more use of St John's. As a result, a group of local people came together to investigate the possibilities and propose a way forward.  It was suggested that the Church of the Holy Saviour at Westbury Leigh might provide a suitable model. In 1999 the nave of this church had been converted into a Community Hall,[6] but the chancel had been retained for worship and partitioned off, although the partition could be opened up for church services. After visiting Westbury Leigh, the group decided to work up a similar project to convert St John's into a community centre.

At its initial meeting in May 2009, the group agreed 'to undertake whatever work was required to secure a future for St. John's by adapting it for wider use by the local community, while retaining a space for worship'.[7] Calling itself Bemerton Community, the group's members were local people who were prepared to dedicate voluntary time and effort to finding a way of preserving St John's, and whose background and skills enabled them to make an effective contribution to the project.  From the outset it was considered fundamental that the group should include the Rector and one of the churchwardens as representatives of Bemerton Parish, so that the project was demonstrably a joint venture.

It was decided to constitute a Core Group to oversee and steer the project, and to put together task teams to manage in detail its three key aspects: converting the building, identifying potential users and raising the necessary finance. The Core Group was also responsible for liaison with the various parties whose support would be important to the project's success: Salisbury Diocese, conservation bodies, local authorities and elected representatives. The need for charitable status was recognised, and so a company limited by guarantee was formed and registered with the Charity Commission, with the Core Group members as directors and trustees.

At this early stage of the project it was not easy to forecast how the building might actually be used and by whom, other than the chancel which would be used by the parish for worship. This made it difficult to decide what conversion work would be involved. However it was evident that the space offered by the nave and side aisles needed to offer as much flexibility of use as possible, and that kitchen and toilet facilities would be essential if the building was to support community activities and at the same time be sufficiently attractive to potential hirers. To allow for shared usage by the parish and the community, the provision of a screen between chancel and nave was felt to be highly desirable.

Also, it proved very difficult at the outset to get any real feel for finance and timescale. Not only were the costings dependent on the extent of the conversion work required, but it was unclear at this stage what professional and planning fees might be involved, and also what repair and maintenance might be needed to the existing fabric. An initial estimate put the overall cost at approximately £350,000. The time needed to complete the project would be governed by the progress in raising this amount, but was considered unlikely to be less than five years.

## Scoping the Project

In July 2009 the PCC took the decision[8] to tell the Diocese formally that it wished to close St. John's for public worship, with the exception of the chancel, and to offer the building to Bemerton Community for use as a local amenity. The way was now clear for the Core Group to conduct a Feasibility Study, examining the scope for alterations to the fabric and interior of the building. The Study also required the production of a Business Plan for the project, in order to justify any proposed changes to the building and to support subsequent efforts to secure financial grants and donations.

To inform the Study about how the local community might wish to use St John's and what facilities they would be looking for, a questionnaire was delivered to 1500 local households, resulting in a return of just over 11%. This was considered enough to guide building priorities, and an initial set of drawings was produced. In September 2009 Bemerton Community presented these proposals to local residents at a second public meeting and they were generally approved, demonstrating popular support for the project.

Views of St John's nave prior to conversion.

The Feasibility Study was also required to take into account any constraints on making alterations to the building. Some of these were practical, such as the limitations on the internal space available within its footprint, and the fact that it was surrounded by a churchyard with a high concentration of graves. Others were restrictions likely to be imposed either by the ecclesiastical authorities or by the various agencies and statutory bodies concerned with conservation.

The importance of involving the various parties concerned with conservation was well appreciated, and during 2010 Bemerton Community arranged briefings in order to gauge their reaction. The initial responses from English Heritage and the Victorian Society were not encouraging; the latter was particularly concerned to preserve St John's as it stood, as a fine example of T H Wyatt's work. An early briefing of the local authority's Conservation Officer also resulted in an unenthusiastic response, essentially because he was not convinced of any need for the building changes involved in order to make it available for community use.

Fortunately this type of situation had been encountered many times by the Church Commissioners, and they were able to produce a Statement of Significance for St John's together with an Informed Change Assessment,[9] which set out a Church of England evaluation of the importance or otherwise of the building's features and content. The two documents provided an effective counter to many of the conservationist concerns and gave Bemerton Community valuable guidance about the opportunities for change. Accordingly, by the end of 2010 the Feasibility Study[10] concluded that the project was potentially viable provided it could be financed, and the decision was made to move towards planning.[11]

The next task was to put together a design brief, setting out the concept and the constraints. In the ensuing discussions with the architect, it became evident that it would not be possible to contain within its existing footprint all the facilities needed to make the building sufficiently flexible and attractive to potential users after conversion. It was decided to add an extension at the north west corner of the church, where it would not be intrusive, and connect it to the nave space by breaking through via the window arch at the west end of the north aisle. The toilets would be situated in the extension, which would also provide wheelchair access and an additional fire exit.

In addition to taking forward the design of the converted building, at this stage it became important to address the issue of how St John's could be leased from Salisbury Diocese once the church had been formally declared redundant. The Church Commissioners advised that the most straightforward arrangement would be for the PCC to take a lease on the chancel, and obtain dispensation for it to remain a consecrated space. Bemerton Community would lease the remainder of the building for non-religious purposes. Following initial meetings with the Diocesan Property Secretary in December 2011, agreement was reached on the outline of the lease, including the division of maintenance responsibilities with the PCC.

The architect considered that the most effective way of producing the detailed drawings needed for planning would be to carry out a laser survey[12] of the building, which would not only provide all the required measurements but would have the added benefit of recording for posterity the details of the church prior to conversion. Also, because the planned provision of kitchen and toilet facilities necessitated gas, water and sewage services being routed through the churchyard to supplement the existing electricity supply, it would be necessary to commission a geophysical survey[13] in order to map the exact location of all the graves. Both surveys were completed in mid-2011.

Armed with the results of the laser survey, the architect was able to produce the first set of detailed drawings of the proposed design. Although these gave rise to considerable discussion within Bemerton Community, leading to some minor changes, there was general agreement that the proposals met the design brief and provided a sound basis for going forward to planning. Unfortunately, even on a rough costing, it was clear that the total cost of conversion was now likely to be in the region of £450,000.

With this cost increase in mind, and given the probability of conservationist objections, in April 2012 it was decided to go through a pre-planning procedure with the local authority[14] in order to identify the most controversial design features and pre-empt potential objections when it came to the formal application for planning agreement. The reaction was disappointingly negative.[15] Although there was acceptance of the need to find a way of preserving the building, it was evident that, unless a very strong case could be made for the alterations shown in the drawings, the planning application would meet significant resistance.

**Funding the Project**

It had been clear from the outset that the project would stand or fall on the ability of Bemerton Community to attract the necessary funds. In the aftermath of the 2008 financial crisis, the fundraising climate was extremely frosty and there was a great deal of competition between charitable bodies and enterprises for increasingly scarce grant funding, especially for amounts in excess of £50,000. It was hardly surprising that, even with some very helpful personal contacts and the engagement of professional fundraisers, applications for major grants were only marginally successful, although some grants did come through in the later stages.

On the other hand, fundraising among the local community had gone well. From the start of the project, Bemerton Community organised various events ranging from a cake stall to an annual carol concert in a very chilly St John's. There were many individual donations, and in the latter stages of the project, local support was most effectively demonstrated by pledged support to the tune of over £70,000. There was also good success with minor grants from local authority sources, mainly for specific aspects of the planning process. However the amounts involved were relatively small. By the end of 2013 it had become increasingly clear that there was a severe funding shortfall and that unless Bemerton Community was able to attract a further £300,000 the project could not go ahead.

It was at this point that Bemerton St John C of E Primary School, situated directly opposite the church, expressed an interest in making regular use of it. In 2004 pupil numbers school had increased by 40% as a result of the change to a two-tier system, resulting in overcrowding of the existing school buildings with no possibility of expansion. This interest opened up the possibility of the school not only renting St John's as its lead tenant, but also attracting capital funding from the Diocesan Board of Education and the Local Education Authority.

Bemerton Community immediately entered into discussions with the school to determine the extent of the usage envisaged, and to examine its impact on the Business Plan. It was agreed that, if the school could have priority call on St John's throughout the day on weekdays during term time, it would be able to enter into a formal agreement to guarantee an annual rental income. It would also provide a justification for capital expenditure of education funds by providing a cost-effective solution to the intractable problem of overcrowding in the existing school buildings. Thus a mutually beneficial way forward emerged, and brought with it £200,000 of additional funding. It also lent considerable weight to the case for conversion, which meant that there could now be more confidence that a planning application would succeed.

## Project Realisation

As there was now a realistic prospect of being able to fund the work needed to convert St John's into a community centre, in January 2014 Bemerton Community took the decision[16] to embark on the formal planning process. The existing draft plans required a small amount of modification to satisfy the school's requirements but no major changes were involved, and so the architect was instructed to produce the final drawings and submit the planning application to the Local Authority. At the same time, the PCC submitted a request to Salisbury Diocese to set in train the Pastoral Measure process in order to satisfy the Church Commissioners.

Although the funding prospects had improved markedly, it was apparent that it would not be possible to complete that project in a single phase. Accordingly, it was decided to split the conversion into three phases, concentrating initially on the work needed to meet the essential requirements of the school. The first phase would cover nave flooring, heating, the kitchen pod and the north aisle breakthrough. The second phase would include the extension building and glass screening of the south aisle. The glass partition between the chancel and the nave would be deferred to the final phase, when it was hoped that more funding sources would be identified.

The project's timescale was effectively governed by the needs of the school, which was expecting to start using St John's with effect from the start of the Autumn Term in September 2015. This would mean that the conversion work would have to begin by no later than April 2015, which allowed a full twelve months for the preparation of the planning application, the application process and the tendering process. The planning application was submitted in May 2014,[17] and at the same time the Diocese began the formal process of declaring the church redundant.

In the event, the planning application process took much longer than anticipated and approval was not granted until October 2014[18] together with listed building consent.[19] Inevitably the approval was conditional on various modifications being made to the planned alterations. Bemerton Community would have preferred to contest some of planning conditions imposed but, sensitive to the need to press on with the project to meet the school's deadline, agreed to compromise. The architect was instructed to make the necessary alterations to the drawings and in February 2015 the tender documents covering the first two phases were sent to three contractors who had expressed an interest in the project. At the same time, arrangements were made to engage a structural engineer to ensure compliance with building regulations.

When the tenders were eventually returned it became clear that Bemerton Community had seriously undervalued the cost of the conversion work, which the estimates put at a minimum of £600,000. The architect was tasked with negotiating with the contractors to find savings in design and materials. At the same time a public appeal was launched in an attempt to cover the cost increase. Fortunately the local community were supportive, but inevitably closing the gap between the cost of the work and the funding available took some time and it was not until September 2015 that the selected contractor was able to begin the conversion, with a completion date scheduled for January 2016.

The first task was renovation of the roof to meet building regulation standards, and to enable internal work to proceed. When the tiles were removed the hitherto unsuspected presence of bats was discovered, and so no further progress could be made until this issue had been reported and resolved. In light of the delay, it was decided to bring the building extension forward into Phase I, resulting in the need to call in an undertaker to move some churchyard graves. This enabled the necessary groundwork for foundations and mains services to be carried out and a start made on construction of the extension. However it gave rise to a further delay and the estimated completion date changed to March 2016.

Meanwhile inside the church the pews and the wooden plinths on which they were mounted had been removed and disposed of, and the contractor was installing the underfloor heating system and levelling the surface prior to the installation of oak flooring. The plain glass window at the west end of the north aisle was removed to provide the breakthrough.to the building extension. To satisfy conservation constraints, the stone slabs removed from the nave were re-laid in the north aisle, and the wooden pod for the kitchen and a small meeting room was installed.

Externally, another problem had emerged; the tower gutter urgently needed replacing. It transpired that the rainwater spout from the tower roof was frequently blocked resulting in water leakage into the vestry. Fortunately this was discovered while the roof scaffolding was still in place, but this gutter work caused yet more delay. Inside the building, work to lay the oak flooring could not be completed until the heating was up and running, and it took some time to get the necessary gas and water services connected. This also enabled the kitchen elements to be installed in the north aisle pod, and the toilets in the

Conversion work in progress, showing the north aisle pod and the breakthrough window.

extension. The conversion project, or at least most of the work envisaged in its first two phases, was eventually completed in May 2016.

## Conclusion

There is no doubt that the conversion of the building, now re-titled St John's Place, has been highly successful. Without losing the essence of T H Wyatt's vision, the interior has been impressively transformed into a clean-looking, brightly lit open space, the breakthrough to the extension building and the extension itself have worked well, and both Bemerton Community and the PCC, who share the maintenance costs, can be confident about the soundness of the fabric. Sufficient additional funds have now been raised to enable the south aisle partition to go ahead, which will complete the second phase of the project and provide an additional separate meeting space with its own access directly from the porch. Bemerton Community is now working to secure funding for the final phase, the full-height glazed partition between the chancel and the nave.

St John's Place was opened officially on 25 June 2016 by John Glen MP. Bemerton Community has appointed a full-time manager and a part-time caretaker. There is a formal agreement with the school, which uses the building daily during term time, and bookings by various activity groups are steadily increasing. It is becoming very popular as a wedding venue, providing as it does a combination of a traditional church setting for the ceremony with excellent facilities for the reception. It is one of the few places available for hire in Salisbury to offer sufficient space for a gathering of up to 180 people.

A project of this type, especially one with strong conservationist interests involved, invariably will encounter difficulties along the way and it was never going to be easy to fund it in the prevailing financial climate. In this case, the solution emerged through partnership with an overcrowded adjacent school although, perhaps inevitably, Bemerton Community underestimated both the timescale to compete the project and its cost.

Nevertheless, the transformation of St John's affords a fine example of what can be achieved with a potentially redundant church building if the local community is sufficiently motivated and determined to preserve its heritage by volunteer effort and innovative thinking.  As Sir Roy Strong put it: 'Not every building without a purpose has a right to live on. The challenge resides in giving them a reason to continue to exist'.[20] In creating St John's Place, Bemerton Community has risen most effectively to that challenge.

**Notes:**

1   Gresham College Special Lecture, *The Beauty of Holiness and its Perils (or what is to happen to 10,000 parish churches?* by Sir Roy Strong, 30 May 2007 (Strong Lecture).
2   Historic England List Entry No 1374113.
3   www.georgeherbert.org.uk visited 3 April 2017.
4   Minutes of Bemerton PCC meeting 11 November 2008.
5   Strong Lecture.
6   www.wvha.org.uk/find-details-page.php?hall_id=333 visited 7 April 2017.
7   Minutes of Bemerton Community Core Group meeting 1 May 2009.
8   Minutes of Bemerton PCC meeting 14 July 2009.
9   Church Buildings Council Informed Change Assessment October 2010.
10  Bemerton Community Feasibility Study 7 December 2010 (revised 22 July 2011).
11  Minutes of Bemerton Community Core Group meeting 22 February 2011.
12  Wessex Archaeology Metric Survey Report Ref. 79120 of November 2011.
13  Wessex Archaeology Ground Penetrating Radar Survey Report Ref. 77780.01 of June 2011.
14  Paul Stevens Architecture PS/CG/445 dated 5 April 2012.
15  Wiltshire Council Development Services PE/2012/0108 dated 18 May 2012.
16  Minutes of Bemerton Community Core Group meeting 16 January 2014.
17  Application for Planning Permission 14/03097/FUL dated 22 April 2014.
18  Notification of Full Planning 14/03097/FUL dated 18 October 2014
19  Notification of Listed Building Consent  14/03097/LBC dated 9 October 2014
20  Strong Lecture.

In the past year since its official opening St John's Place has hosted daily school activities, a much needed after school club and holiday play scheme, weddings, baptisms, regular film showings, many private parties for children and sophisticated evening gatherings for adults, as well as regular sessions for older people and sadly two memorial services for early supporters of the project events. A wild flower area has been seeded as part of the greening of the churchyard, working with children from the school. After a year of operation the project seems to be viable, with funds being transferred to a sinking fund for future repairs, and the community has an asset to be proud of. Here is the first Bemerton Brunch which brought that community together across the ages on a Sunday morning. Photo and caption Anne Trevett.

The northern range viewed from Crane St, as depicted by John Buckler 1805, DZ.SWS:1982.767 © Wiltshire Museum, Devizes. 2017 photo by Roy Bexon

# Church House

## Andrew Minting and Ruth Newman

*This is the first of what it is hoped will be a series of articles on the history of influential buildings in the city, including both architecture and residents.*

Church House, previously known as Audley House, is a fine Grade 1 listed building, one of the rare medieval stone houses in the city.[1] With its extensive façade in Crane Street it fronts one of the oldest thoroughfares in Salisbury stretching east along New Street in a straight line right through to Payne's Hill.

Home of a rich city wool merchant in the mid 15th century, the house possibly received a visit from Henry VIII and Anne Boleyn in 1535, and was associated with a 17th century sexual scandal. In a reversal of fortune it acted as the city workhouse for 242 years experiencing a particular tragedy in the mid 19th century with the avoidable death of a young child.[2] From 1881 it became the Diocesan Church House and today contains the offices of the diocese.

### William Lightfoot

The house dates from the mid 15th century and was probably the property, 'Le Faucon', owned by William Lightfoot in 1455, where he would have displayed his trade sign, the falcon or hawk. He owned three houses in Salisbury, and a meadow with tentering racks[3] near St Martin's Church. A man of national importance, owning property in Essex and Suffolk as well as Wiltshire, he acted as city mayor in 1451–2 and later as an MP. He was one of a group of powerful Salisbury merchants including John Halle, William Swayne, John Wyot and John à Porte.[4] With other wealthy citizens he sponsored the rebuilding of St Thomas's Church, advertising his philanthropy with his merchant's mark which can be seen in the south chapel. Another shield in the same chapel has been ascribed to former mayor John Wyot and his mark also appears on a corbel in the hall of Church House.[5] During Lightfoot's mayoralty it was

# CHURCH HOUSE *Crane Street*

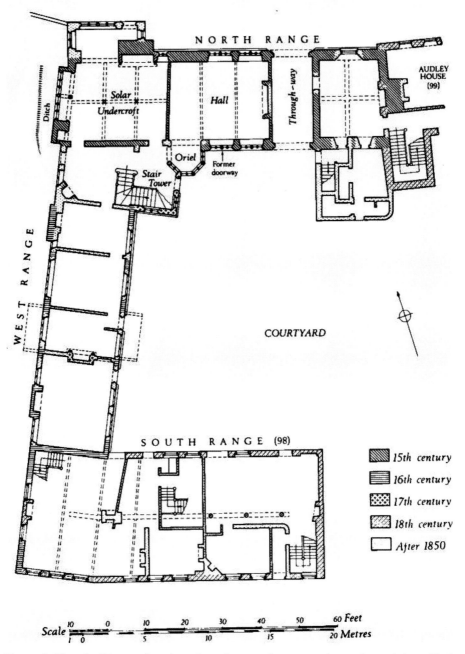

Plan of Church House showing the phases of construction of surviving fabric, reproduced from RCHME *Salisbury* Volume I p74 (HMSO, 1980). © Crown Copyright, Historic England Archive.

agreed in February 1452 that the prostitutes 'were to be removed from Culver Street ("Colverstrete") to outside the city and not to enter the city . . . for any length of time . . . except they come in the striped hoods prescribed for them on pain of imprisonment'. He also supervised the cleansing of the streets and water channels ordering that the sewers and gutters should be 'so cleansed and repaired they may be kept in their state of well-being to the adornment of the city'.[6]

Salisbury was a great trading centre in the 15th century for the woollen cloth industry. A flourishing cosmopolitan trade linked the city with Southampton. William Lightfoot exported woollen cloth to France and Italy but imported a huge range of luxuries including almonds, rice, spices, dates, sugar, wax and paper, as well as dyes and alum for industrial use. In just a few months in 1444 his wagons arrived in Salisbury from Southampton with 20 gallons of olive oil, 1½ tons of fruit and 250 gallons of wine.[7] He was probably the builder in the mid 15th century of the northern range fronting Crane Street.

The property comprises three distinct sections around an open courtyard, its eastern side undeveloped and abutting the gardens of 97 Crane St, the 18th century dwelling now known as Audley House. The northern range dates from the mid 15th century, the western the mid 16th, and the southern mid 18th, with varying degrees of alteration and addition since.[8]

The northern range's Crane Street frontage provides access to the yard through a large 15th century arched gateway with rooms and original windows over, bearing some stylistic similarities with the major gateways through the cathedral close wall. The carved and panelled oak gates retain much of their original timber. To the east of the gate (left as viewed from the road) are rooms that served as domestic accommodation and retain 18th century sash windows at first floor level; these had been annexed by 95 Crane St and were restored to Church House ownership in 1890.[9] To the west lies a medieval hall with heavily restored timber framed end walls and a three-bay arch-braced timber roof with moulded trusses and highly unusual trefoil-headed open panels.[10] The trusses spring from stone corbels

The merchant's mark of John Wyot on a corbel in the medieval hall, photo by Roy Bexon

Heavy timber framing exposed in the medieval hall, photo by Roy Bexon

carved with angels and other figures; one of these has a merchant's mark now attributed to John Wyot, the long-held belief that it was John Webb's having been discounted. At the north western corner of the courtyard, stands a 17th century stairtower that partially encloses an original oriel window, providing access to the hall's gallery, although this appears to be a 19th century creation.

At the western end of the hall lies the solar and its undercroft. The first floor solar retains a 16th century geometric ribbed plaster ceiling and nearly all of its original moulded joinery and the only surviving original fireplace, of stone with three large carved quatrefoils. The bay that projects into Crane St was rebuilt in the late 19th century. Privies in the western wall at ground and first floor level (the latter probably removed in the 1880s), drained into the Close ditch fed from the river Avon. The undercroft was in use as the workhouse brewhouse in 1742.[11]

The next known occupant was Thomas Coke (1455-1523), merchant and mayor and by reputation the wealthiest person in the city. On his

The outlet from the medieval privy discharged into what remains of the Cathedral Close ditch. It is still visible from the garden on the western side, photo by Andrew Minting

death he bequeathed the house to his daughter Scholastica, the wife of Thomas Chafyn who probably added the new west wing and enlarged the courtyard sometime after 1523.

The two storeyed western range is of brick under a tiled roof. This wing has been altered the most of the three, having been almost rebuilt in the late 19th century and further altered since – some early brickwork may be seen in both its elevations, however much is later replacement, including all the brick chimney stacks. The oak-framed mullioned windows with geometric leaded lights date from the late 19th century, although it is likely that they are near-replicas of earlier windows in the building; small panels of painted glass by W G Randall dated 1950 have been inserted into the first floor window at the south western corner of the yard.[12]

Church House, west range, extensively altered in the 1880s but retaining some 16th century features, © Peter Higginbotham/workhouses.org.uk

## Possible visit of Henry VIII and Anne Boleyn[13]

Thomas Chafyn was definitely in possession of the house in 1547 (when he was mayor) but he might have sublet the property between 1523 and 1547, in which case it is just feasible that Lord Audley received Henry VIII there in 1535.

The king visited Salisbury with Anne Boleyn in October 1535 when a magnificent reception was planned.[14] Sir Anthony Wyndesore wrote to Lord Lisle on 9 October confirming that Henry was in Hampshire, as part of the Royal Progress, from 10 September to 19 October 1535, 'except 4 days that his Grace lieth in Salisbury'. While in the vicinity the royal couple visited Clarendon Park, hunting and hawking in one of the finest medieval deer parks in the country. They appear to have been guests in Salisbury of John Tuchet (Touchet), 8th Baron Audley.[15] In a letter written from Salisbury to Thomas Cromwell on 10 October 1535 he wrote, 'my trust is that the King's highness and the Queen's grace hath been meetly well content with their poor lodging in my rude house'. The dwelling in question was ostensibly the present day Church House and the name 'Audley House' might date back to this visit rather than to his notorious descendant, the 12th Lord Audley (see below). If this assertion is correct the royal couple would have lodged in the recently built western range (early 16th century) and in the 15th century solar. During his stay in the city Henry decided that the two year old princess Elizabeth was old enough to be weaned. Sir William Paulet, the Comptroller of the Royal Household, wrote to Thomas Cromwell from Salisbury on 9 October, 'the King having considered the letter to Cromwell, [originally sent by Anne] . . . has decided that she [Elizabeth] shall be weaned with all diligence'. So, it is possible that such domestic matters were discussed at Church House, an interesting insight into the welfare of the future Queen.[16]

From c1559 the house belonged to Piers Harris and by 1578 had been bought by John Bayley of Bishopsdown. In 1630 his heirs sold the house to Mervyn Touchet, Lord Audley, 2nd Earl of Castlehaven (c1593−1631).[17]

## Early 17th century scandal

Touchet's notoriety was infamous in the early 17th century and he was associated with a sensational sexual scandal of 1631. He succeeded his father in about 1617, living at Fonthill Gifford but using Church House as his town house. His sexual excesses appear to have taken place in both houses. He was committed in December 1630 and charged with assisting in the rape of his second wife, the Countess, and two charges of sodomy with his manservants. By mid March 1631 the formal process of indicting and trying the Earl was underway. The King (Charles I) set up a commission in Salisbury headed by Edward, Lord Gorges from Longford Castle, with a Grand Jury to hear the Crown's evidence. He was indicted, with the trial before his fellow peers taking place at Westminster Hall on 25 April. It attracted enormous publicity, the trial of a peer being rare even without the extreme nature of the supposed crimes. He always protested his innocence but was unanimously convicted of rape, and a majority of jurors (15 out of 26) found him guilty of the two charges of sodomy. In reality the most damning evidence against him was that he encouraged 'riotous' behaviour in the household that he, as an earl, was meant to be protecting. His suspected Roman Catholic allegiance did nothing to help his case. The Attorney General stated that, 'by being a Protestant in the Morning and a Papist in the Afternoon, no wonder if he commits the most abominable Impieties'.[18] As a nobleman he was beheaded (rather than hanged) on Tower Hill on 14 May 1631 for 'unnatural offences'. His two manservants were sentenced to death by hanging a few months later.[19]

His property was confiscated and divided between the bishop, as Lord of the Manor, and the Earl's heir, who sold his share to William Collis, a member of the city council. The Corporation bought out Collis and the bishop granted his portion ('moiety') in order that the building could be used as the city workhouse and house of correction, the transaction finally taking place in September 1637.

## City Workhouse 1637-1879

Church House was thus established as the city workhouse, serving the city parishes of St Thomas's, St Edmund's and St Martin's for 242 years, until 1879 – an historical fate unimaginable to its earlier residents.[20]

The 1630s were years of severe unemployment, partly because of a contraction in the woollen cloth industry at home and abroad. The new workhouse originally housed just 16 boys and 14 girls 'not beinge Bastards'. It was a conventional institution, the children wearing badges with the arms of the city and distinctive blue caps, far removed from the progressive Puritan schemes of the early 17th century.[21]

Every part of the building was used for the workhouse. The southern range dates from 1728 and is of three storeys of red brick under a tiled roof and an unusually deep moulded cornice. The simplified Classical treatment has stone plat-bands and keystones between the floors, and each floor has nine aligned 12-pane sliding sash windows, bar those lost on the ground floor to two plain doorways. This block was built by the city to provide extra accommodation for the workhouse, with its ground floor marked as 'workshop' on a plan of 1742, supporting the dormitories above.[22]

Increasingly after 1800 the poor relief system came under pressure with population growth, and the inflationary impact of the long wars against France. With over 2000 in poverty in the city and rapidly rising rates, the institution was increasingly criticised as it failed to cope with the sheer numbers of those in distress. Henry Wansey, a Warminster clothier, in a damning report of 1801, described the Crane Street workhouse as inefficiently managed and

Church House, south range, built 1728 as an enlargement to the workhouse. It housed the workshop with dormitories above. © Peter Higginbotham/workhouses.org.uk

overcrowded.[23] Little had changed by 1834 when it was stated, in the Poor Law Report, that the inspector had 'never seen a more disgusting scene of filth and misrule.'[24]

The subsequent Act combined parishes into Unions under elected Boards of Guardians and established the 'well regulated' workhouse to act as a deterrent, believing that only the genuinely desperate would apply for relief.[25]

The three city parishes had already joined together by an Act of 1770 to share rates and administer relief; despite criticism, they remained as a 'Union' with their own Board of Guardians in Crane Street, largely exempt from the terms of the 1834 Act.[26]

The city workhouse continued to receive a bad press. Thomas Rammell's report on the sanitary condition of Salisbury 1851, following the cholera outbreak two years earlier, described the building as 'unfitting' with an open privy and 'very defective as to ventilation'. Four deaths were recorded in 1849 from cholera.[27]

It was against this background of disapproval that a particularly tragic scandal broke in 1856 – the death of an innocent young child. It was reported in the *Salisbury Journal* that nine year old Louisa (Sophia) Garrett had died at the workhouse on the 5 June, shortly after being taken out of a sulphur bath, used 'for the cure of persons afflicted with the itch'.[28] Even the Christian name of the young pauper girl seemed uncertain, compounding the tragedy.[29] The inquest was held two days later. The bath had been used without medical supervision and Sophia had been left immersed for at least 35 minutes.[30] She called for water, went black in the face and died shortly after. The medical officer, Dr John Winzar,[31] confirmed that the child had died from being left too long in the contraption – that ten minutes were sufficient. The post mortem concluded that the child had died from 'congestion of the brain' and the case was reported to the Poor Law Commissioners in London and was followed by an inquiry overseen by a Poor Law inspector and held at the Salisbury Workhouse.[32] The investigation provides an unusual insight into life in the Crane Street institution in the mid 19th century.[33]

The above details were reported in the *Salisbury Journal* but the National Archives revealed further evidence which the local paper omitted. The central Poor Law Board was very critical of Dr John Winzar, in that he did not know his patients, did not visit regularly, did not inspect the sulphur bath and was 'remiss in the discharge of his duties . . . and deserves a severe reprimand'. Indeed the catastrophe was attributed to the negligence of the Medical Officer and the ignorance of the workhouse officials including the schoolmistress who had been supervising the bath on the day, refused to give Sophia water and used her cane to try to rouse her.[34]

Continued bad press led to its demise. The Salisbury and Alderbury Unions amalgamated in 1869 and a new enlarged structure for 400 paupers was built in 1877-1879 on the Coombe Road site. After 242 years, in 1879, the workhouse in Crane Street finally closed, the paupers moving the following year to their new 'home', renamed officially the Salisbury Union Workhouse in 1895.[35]

**Conversion from workhouse to Church House**

Church House now entered its final phase. Archdeacon Thomas Sanctuary led the campaign to find new accommodation for various inadequately housed functions of the diocese, acquiring the site from its two owners, the city council and the Ecclesiastical Commissioners for £1500 in 1881, later signing ownership over to the Diocesan Board of Finance in 1886. He immediately established the Church House Committee to determine the functions the site would serve and the necessary changes to facilitate them, including two libraries (one endowed by Miss Chafyn Grove), a board room, committee rooms, space for the SPCK bookshop, missionary facilities, and accommodation for the caretaker. Audley House, with the rooms above and to the east of the gateway which served this last purpose, was purchased for £1100 in 1890.[36]

Sanctuary, who was from Dorset, proposed the well-known Dorset architect George Crickmay to carry out the necessary repairs and alterations, and gave clear instructions, supported by the Dean, that he should 'preserve every ancient feature, removing only when necessary such parts as were evidently erected or altered in recent times'.[37]

A condition of the sale of the city's portion of the freehold had been that a projection into Crane St, two small rooms marked as 'tramp house' on a plan commissioned from local architect Alfred Bothams, should be demolished immediately in order that the access to Crane Bridge be widened.[38] This may have prompted the extensive rebuilding of that part of the hall, the only part of the site to have a distinctly late-Victorian character.

The hall had endured several insertions including a first floor in the early 17th century, and it is believed the windows had been altered to serve these better. The illustrations by Twopeny and Buckler show a pair of four-light cinquefoil-headed windows in the position of the lower sections of the windows we see today, with similarly sized windows tucked under the eaves and a band of masonry in between.[39] After removal of the floor, the Church House Committee resolved in 1883 that Crickmay should rearrange the windows in the southern elevation, and a year later that the northern side should be altered to match. It appears that during these works, which would have required significant disturbance to both elevations, the southern side, where an early doorway was also removed and infilled, was refaced with broken flint instead of ashlar.[40] During the following few years, a possibly unparalleled collection of 14th and 15th century stone fireplaces was assembled in Church House by donations from several sources, including a house in Mere belonging to Miss Chafyn Grove, and two from the Earl of Radnor. One had even been found in 1788 on the site of the Bishop's Guildhall.[41]

In 1892, the south range was restored by Crickmay for use by the St Andrew's Missioners, and a lease granted for 14 years. In 1924, however, it was converted to residential use, as it remains today, with rented apartments and ground floor office space.[42]

During the conversion Archbishop Sanctuary held 'a pleasant conversazione' for the wedding of Maude Hamilton, the daughter of the late Bishop, with the Rev E B Ottley. The workmen's tools were hidden and the fires 'blazed away' as the fine mansion underwent the transition from the 'dilapidated city "workus", to use Oliver Twist's word, to an ecclesiastical head-quarters.'[43] This

The northern range viewed from within the courtyard looking west, as depicted by John Buckler 1805, DZ.SWS:1982.768 © Wiltshire Museum, Devizes. 2017 photo by Roy Bexon

final 'transition' has proved to be enduring; it is believed to be the first such church house in the country and in 2017 it remains in diocesan use.[44]

## Acknowledgements

Thanks are due to Alex Weedon for her time and enthusiasm in showing the authors around Church House; and to Margaret Scard for her expert advice on details concerning Henry VIII and his visit to Salisbury in October 1535.

## Abbreviations and notes

SJ = *Salisbury and Winchester Journal*

RCHME = Royal Commission on the Historical Monuments of England, 1980, *City of Salisbury,* HMSO

TNA = The National Archives

WSA = Wiltshire and Swindon Archives

WAM = Wiltshire Archaeological Magazine

## Notes

1 Another medieval stone house in the city was John Halle's banqueting hall, the foyer to the current Odeon cinema.

2 William Naish's map of Salisbury published in 1751 shows the building as 'workhouse and bridewell'.

3 After fulling, the wet cloth was stretched and dried on wooden-framed tentering racks: Rogers, Kenneth, 2016, 'The rack houses on Milford Hill', *Sarum Chronicle* 16, 149-50.

4 Everett, C R, *Wiltshire Archaeological Magazine*, XLIX (1941).

5 It is just possible that Wyot rather than Lightfoot may have been responsible for the original building.

6 Carr, David R, (ed) (2001), *The First General entry Book of the City of Salisbury* 1387-1452, Wiltshire Record Society, vol 54, 241, 242.

7 Harwood, W A (ed), *The Southampton Brokage Book, 1447-48*, Southampton Records Series, 42 (Southampton, 2008); Harwood, Winifred A, Southampton's brokage books and Salisbury, *Sarum Chronicle* 10, 49; Chandler, John, *Endless Street,* 82-3.

8 RCHME *Salisbury* vol 1, 73-76.

9 WSA D370/1

10 The panels sit near the top of the A-frames, or trusses, trefoils having three cusps, a little like a clover leaf, usually set within the top of a Gothic arch and imbued with Christian significance.

11 RCHME *Salisbury* vol 1, 73-76, plate 12.

12 The geometric leaded light pattern matches that found on the south elevation of Bishop Wordsworth's School, 11 The Close.

13 Much of this section is speculative although recent research appears to suggest that it is possible.

14 Hatcher, Henry, 1843, *Old and New Sarum or Salisbury,* by Robert Benson and Henry Hatcher, London: Nichols, 236-7, quoting from the City muniments Ledger B, fol.

280. There are no records of a grand ceremony coinciding with the 1535 royal visit to Salisbury.

15  John Tuchet (Touchet), 8th Baron Audley (1483-1557). James Harris in 1825, *Copies of epitaphs in Salisbury Cathedral* wrote that 'the [Audley] family mansion for many years was the house in Crane-Street, Salisbury, now used as a workhouse': https://books.google.co.uk/books?id=q7cHAAAAQAAJ: accessed 17.02.17.

16  Collins, Brian M, 2011, 'The Reformation and St Swithuns Priory: as told by the contemporary sources for 1535, The Royal Progress and Anne Boleyn's Visit to Winchester in 1535'. **https://www.winchester-cathedral.org.uk/.../The-Reformation-and-St-Swithuns-Priory: accessed** 15.02.17. Morris, Sarah and Grueninger, Natalie, 2013, *In the footsteps of Anne Boleyn,* Amberley, 255-60.

17  Mervyn Touchet was the 12th Lord Audley in the English peerage and the 2nd Lord Audley and 2nd Earl of Castlehaven in the peerage of Ireland (Wikipedia).

18  Quoted in Norton, Rictor, 2009, 'The Trial of Mervyn Touchet, Earl of Castlehaven, 1631', *Gay History and Literature.* http://rictornorton.co.uk/touchet.htm, accessed 17.02.2017. In recent years the case has received publicity as an interesting historic case of an early trial concerning homosexuality.

19  Ferris, John P and Hunneyball, Paul, 2010, 'Audley, alias Tuchet, Sir Mervyn (c.1588-1631) . . . of Fonthill Gifford, Wilts', *The History of Parliament.* Herrup, Cynthia B. 2004, 'Touchet, Mervin, second earl of Castlehaven (1593–1631)'. *Oxford Dictionary of National Biography* (online ed), Oxford University Press. (Subscription or UK public library membership required.)

20  Much of the following section is taken from Newman, Ruth, 2014, 'A 19th century workhouse scandal', *Sarum Chronicle* 14, 71-81.

21  John Ivie, Puritan mayor in the 1620s, introduced an ambitious plan to try to eliminate the underlying causes of poverty: Slack, P, 1975, *Poverty in Early Stuart Salisbury,* Wiltshire Record Society, 31, 9-14; Newman, R & Howells, J, 2001, *Salisbury Past,* Phillimore, 41-44.

22  RCHME, *Salisbury* vol 1, 73 and plate 12.

23  Wansey, Henry, 1801, *Thoughts on Poor-Houses, with a view to their general reform, as applicable to Salisbury,* passim.

24  *Poor Law Commission Report* (1834), App A, Pt I, 8a-9a; *VCH Wilts,* 5, 253, note 60.

25  Poor Law Amendment Act (1834): Newman & Howells, 78.

26  A new Alderbury Union workhouse at the junction of the Coombe and Odstock roads, south of the city, was built in 1836, as a direct result of the Poor Law Amendment Act, accommodating up to 200 paupers from the Close and 21 other local parishes: Newman & Howells, 78; www.workhouses.org.uk/Alderbury/, accessed 2014.

27  Rammell, Thomas, 1851, *Report of the General Board of Health on a preliminary inquiry into the sewerage, drainage and supply of water, and the sanitary condition of the inhabitants of the city and borough of Salisbury, in the county of Wilts.* London: HMSO, 13-15.

28  *SJ,* 7 June 1856, 3; sulphur springs had long been recognised for their therapeutic properties in treating skin conditions. Suphur ointment had been used to treat 'the itch' (probably a form of scabies) before the use of the sulphur bath.

29  The first report (7 June) in the *Salisbury Journal* referred to 'Louisa'. By 21 June 'Louisa' had become 'Sophia' and the 1851 census confirms that this was her correct name. What particular tragedy had led young Sophia to be in the workhouse has been impossible to

trace.

30 The bath was described as a large box with a hole in the lid for the head.

31 John Winzar (1805-76) was well known in Salisbury's 19th-century medical history.

32 *Salisbury Journal,* 7 June 1856, 3, *SJ,* 14 June 1856, 3, *SJ,* 21 June 1856, 4.

33 Newman, Ruth, 'A 19th century workhouse scandal', *Sarum Chronicle* 14, 2014, 71-81.

34 TNA, MH 12/13847: Corres. 1834-1869 (Salisbury).

35 www.workhouses.org.uk/Alderbury/, accessed 2017.

36 WSA D/370/1, D370/2.

37 WSA D/370/2; *SJ* 30 April 1881.

38 WSA D370/1; G23/116/1.

39 RCHME *Salisbury* vol 1, plates 9, 11.

40 It is unknown why the original stone could not be salvaged and reused but it may have suffered more from the weather than the northern side, and the cost of its replacement deemed excessive, or perhaps it was an early nod to the principles of 'honest repair' of the Society for the Protection of Ancient Buildings, whose interest in the building had been aroused when the city had proposed its demolition after the workhouse had relocated.

41 *WAM* xxxvi (1910), 370-2; RCHME, *Salisbury* vol 1, 75, 76 plates 90, 91.

42 WSA D370/2.

43 *Salisbury Times*, 26 January 1884, 8; 27 December 1884, 8.

44 The site was requisitioned by the War Department 1916-20 as additional offices for Southern Command based at Radnor House in Salisbury.

# St Thomas's Festivals

## John Cox

St Thomas's Church from the north. (Photo by Roy Bexon)

At Easter 1980 an appeal was launched by St Thomas's Church in Salisbury for the restoration of stonework of the tower. Within three years sufficient funds had been raised to pay for the necessary work and also refacing the clock and overhauling its jacks[1]. Among the many events that contributed to the success of the appeal was an ambitious venture in the summer of 1981. With the enthusiastic support of the Rector of St Thomas, the Venerable Nigel McCulloch, and St Thomas's PCC, I undertook to direct a Festival of Arts and Crafts in the church. This was to coincide with the annual week of patronal festivals in honour of St Thomas of Canterbury and St Edmund of Abingdon, following the union of St Edmund's and St Thomas's parishes in 1973, when the Church of St Edmund was made redundant and became Salisbury Arts Centre.

The programme for the Festival aimed to cover a wide range of performing and visual arts and feature a diversity of professional and amateur artists, of both local and national standing. While it was hoped participants might waive or reduce fees and expenses in supporting the restoration of a beautiful medieval building, common sense required a search for sponsorship and donations to offset costs and maximise proceeds. Compared with more recent economically straitened times, local businesses were able and willing to help by donations or by payment for advertising space in programmes. The most substantial sponsorship came from UK Provident, then a major employer in Salisbury, and there was generous support of various kinds from other businesses, the appeal patrons and well-wishers.

A key figure in securing exhibitions of a high quality was the late Bill Toop[2]. He arranged and mounted a range of work by the artist and cartoonist Norman Thelwell. This delighted the fans of his plump ponies and intrigued people who had not seen his wider range of subjects. Bill also exhibited his own very popular watercolours of Salisbury scenes, and judged a children's art competition.

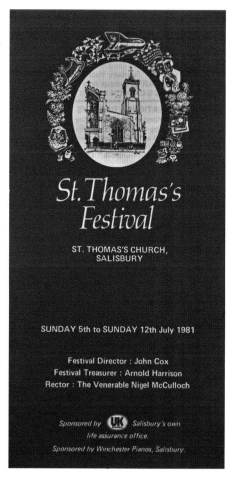

Cover of the 1981 St Thomas's Festival leaflet.

Local photographer and self-build camera designer Hugh Jackson completed the range of displays. Throughout the week there were also demonstrations by embroiderers, flower arrangers and lace-makers, as well as work in enamelling, iron and pottery. My father's retirement activity of chair caning was on show, though he was nonplussed when one visitor came expecting a demonstration of choir caning… Trips up the tower, not usually open to the public, proved popular in providing visitors with a panorama of the roofscape of Salisbury's centre, and the quality of refreshments on sale was likewise widely appreciated.

The four evening events included two recitals. The harpist Marisa Robles made a triumphant return after her appearance at the previous year's Salisbury Festival. Her music-making was peerless and her introductions charmingly informative. The other recital was by the pianist Rosalind Runcie, better known to many as the wife of Robert, then Archbishop of Canterbury. Though more often a teacher than a performer she delivered fine performances of music of three centuries. Words and music on the theme of *Summers Old and New* were appropriately performed at the end of the week of beautiful weather by the Farrant Singers, conducted by Richard Shephard, with the actors Charmian May and Sonia Woolley, well-known to audiences at Salisbury Playhouse.

Words of a very different kind came in what for many was the high point of the Festival as well as being a sell-out: Alec McCowen[3] in his solo performance of St Mark's Gospel in the Authorised Version. Delivering the whole book from memory on a virtually bare stage he mesmerised his audience as he had done in performances across the world in very different venues. He not only conveyed the drama and emotion of the text but also shared unexpected moments of humour and pathos. His glass of water on a table was his one prop – and a judicious drink at one point coincided with the appearance of Herod who came over as very fond of a drop or two of whisky. The shifting sunlight of a summer's evening across the Doom Painting on the chancel arch provided a perfect setting for the passing of time in the Gospel.

Perhaps it was a case of beginners' luck, but the Festival was successful for what it delivered and for the excess of £6,000 raised for the Appeal, which then seemed a very substantial amount. We were blessed not only with good support from so many people but with degrees of good luck. Any organiser of such an event knows you can be on thin ice at times and have to act decisively as when we called on Robert Glazebrook at Steinway & Sons. To our immense gratitude he supplied at very short notice a concert grand and tuner when our original supplier was unable to deliver. At other times you have just to hope for the best as I did when giving Alec McCowen his ten minute call and found him on his knees in the rectory looking over the carpet for a lost contact lens – which he found in good time and with professional calm then proceeded to the stage.

In the 1981 concert programmes Nigel McCulloch concluded his introduction with these words:

> What you see here also represents the wide range of activities and talents among our own members, from young to old. They belong to a growing congregation which is determined to pass on this glorious church and the faith for which it has so long stood to future generations of Salisbury citizens.

That same determination continued during the 1980s as a further Appeal was launched, this time to repair crumbling stonework on the north face of the church. At that time the Department of the Environment pledged matched funding, so that every pound raised was effectively doubled. The continuing need for fund-raising led to two further Festivals, in 1983 and 1985, which I had the pleasure and the privilege of directing.

The programmes followed the pattern of the first Festival with some developments. The Salisbury Local History Group undertook the tower tours, and a wider range of craft demonstrations included brass rubbing, ceramic conservation, macramé, marquetry, and wood carving.

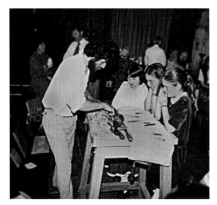

Axel Keim demonstrating wood carving in the 1983 Festival.

The Ven. Nigel McCulloch, Rector of St Thomas's, and Peter Dalton, Mayor of Salisbury, viewing demonstrations in the 1983 Festival.

To complement the work of spinners and weavers for one Festival there was the additional appearance of Coco, a large adult ram owned (and loaned) by Michael Snell whose chocolate shop and tea rooms then faced St. Thomas's. Coco grazed peacefully in his shady pen near the west entrance, unaware of the outraged member of a self-styled animals' vigilante group. Her complaint to me that the animal was being treated inhumanely was directed to his owner. Michael Snell succinctly explained that Coco as a mature male was usually kept in isolation from other animals for most of the time and was equally accustomed to human attention. Another complaint came from a passing

Katie Stewart and ladies in the 1983 Festival.

Portuguese woman who was outraged that her language was not among the many featured in a welcome sign to visitors. 'How can you treat your oldest ally in this way?' A reconciliation was reached when she agreed to give us the correct wording in her language to add to the sign.

An innovation to the programme was the inclusion of cookery, rightfully taking its place among the arts and crafts even though producing more ephemeral creations. The demonstrations by Katie Stewart (1983) and Mary Berry (1985) were very popular, each expert well-known at the time for their work in magazines. Katie Stewart was cookery editor for *Woman's Journal* before

Robert Key MP, Julian Wiltshire and Bill Toop in the 1985 Festival looking at Bill Toop's watercolour painting of the nave and Doom Painting of St Thomas's.

she moved to *The Times*, and Mary Berry was then more to be found in the issues of *Family Circle* than on television.

The art exhibitions maintained a high standard, largely due to Bill Toop's continuing organisation. These included works by Sir Hugh Casson, David Shepherd, the Royal Institute of Painters and Watercolour, and the Society of Equestrian Artists. In the 1983 Festival Bill demonstrated his artistry in his water colour painting of the nave and Doom Painting of St Thomas's, and a year later a limited print edition of this was available, a percentage of the sales benefitting the church.

*The Head of Christ* by Elisabeth Frink.

In 1983 Dame Elisabeth Frink very generously responded to my request to take part in the 1983 Festival by not only loaning a range of her sculptures but also arranging their transport and setting up. Among the items the monumental *Bronze Head of Christ* looked down upon the maquette of the *Shepherd with his Flock*, the full version of which is now in Paternoster Square near St Paul's Cathedral.

Each Festival again included four evening events. Among the highlights were two concerts by the Allegri String Quartet, the second time with the veteran clarinettist Jack Brymer in works by Weber and Mozart. Geraldine McEwan, fresh from her superb Mrs Proudie in the BBC's *Barchester Chronicles*, performed her delightful solo Jane Austen entertainment, *Two Inches of Ivory*. The concluding Festival concerts became a tradition, with the Farrant Singers conducted by Colin Walsh, and Sonia Woolley joined by David Horlock, Artistic Director of the Playhouse at the time. They performed programmes of words and music celebrating Salisbury in *A Very Brave Place* and summertime in *The River Glideth at His Own Sweet Will*.

With the ongoing support of local sponsorship and individual donations, over £13,000 was raised by these later Festivals, and so the Appeal was brought to a successful conclusion. The Appeal Chairman, Willi Verdon-Smith, paid tribute in 1985 not only to all those who had worked in the preparation and organisation of the Festival but to the other craftsmen involved in the restoration 'who worked tirelessly through the last extremely cold winter – the workmanship is a joy to see.'

The weekly services were carried on throughout the Festivals and it was appropriate and rewarding that preachers included priests with particular links to the church among them Canon Edward Brooks, Nigel McCulloch's predecessor as Rector, and the Dean of Salisbury, the Very Reverend Sidney Evans, a patron of St. Thomas's.

A further seven Festivals of a modified kind continued until 1997 in aid of other restoration work at the church. They drew more upon local participants and were prudently programmed to limit costs in the face of declining sources of sponsorship. Nonetheless they continued to be a vibrant part of St Thomas's ministry as the city centre church of Salisbury, opening its doors to thousands of visitors as well as its own members to share in the celebration of human creativity in a holy place. The annual Christmas Tree Festivals at St Thomas's in the first week of Advent continue this rich tradition, and as I write implementation of the major Redevelopment Plan continues, following the installation of the glass doors and the porch at the west entrance. Further fund-raising is in view.

*opposite page*
Bill Toop's print of the nave and Doom Painting of St Thomas's Church.

# Notes

1. Below the clock face are two figures or 'jacks' one metre high. They each hold a halberd and they rotate at each quarter and simulate hitting the bells, although in fact they do not. The bells are actually struck by hammers from behind. The Jacks represent men in late 16th century armour.

2. From the website of the Royal Institute of Painters in Water Colours (accessed 17.2.17): 'It is with much sadness and deep regret that we have to tell you that Bill Toop RI passed away suddenly on 30th December 2016. Born in 1943 in Bere Regis, Dorset, Bill had a long career in the Arts and Education, opening his own gallery in Wiltshire in 1976, later moving the gallery premises to Dorset. Bill exhibited widely and worked as an illustrator for many publishers.'

3. Alec McCowen died on 6 February 2017, aged 91. He was most widely known for his stage roles in classical and contemporary theatre. His solo performance of St Mark's Gospel was first performed in 1978, and over several years he received international acclaim. He was delighted after a performance given for President Jimmy Carter to have a review entitled *A White Horse Performance*. At a reception after another performance in the USA in a large auditorium, a wealthy and short-sighted patron swept past him and flung her arms in rapturous appreciation around Alec McCowen's bemused technician.

# Vaughan Williams and Salisbury

## John Chandler

Ralph Vaughan Williams was almost a Wiltshireman. Down Ampney vicarage, where he was born in 1872, stands 470 metres from Gloucestershire's boundary with Wiltshire.[1] But his connection with the county, indeed with Salisbury, began even before he was born, and continued until within days of his death in 1958. Arthur, his father, served as curate at Bemerton between 1860 and 1863, and so would have been closely involved in the completion and early ministry of St John's Church, which was dedicated in 1860.[2] Ralph hardly knew his father, by all accounts a saintly Victorian churchman, since he died

in 1875 when his son was little more than two years old. But the Bemerton affinity cannot have escaped the young composer when in 1911 he composed *Five Mystical Songs* for baritone, choir and orchestra, settings of poems by George Herbert, his father's illustrious predecessor in the parish. A few years earlier, in 1869, Arthur's brother Edward had been presented to the rectory of North Tidworth, and there he remained for over 40 years. As a child Ralph holidayed with his uncle. He was taken to see the Tidworth ringers practising, and was allowed to call the numbers of the changes.[3]

Another family connection brought Ralph to the area as a man in his twenties. In 1897 he married

Adeline Vaughan Williams in 1908 (BL MS Mus 1714/10/4, reproduced by kind permission of the Vaughan Williams Charitable Trust).

Adeline Fisher, granddaughter of a canon of Salisbury, who was related to the painter John Constable's friend, Bishop Fisher.[4] Her parents inherited a house at Brockenhurst in the New Forest, where Adeline grew up, and where her father was buried in 1903.[5] Later that year, in July, Ralph and Adeline holidayed with her mother in Salisbury, went boating on the Avon and visited Stonehenge.[6] During another holiday, in 1904, Ralph spent a few days in the Salisbury area collecting folk songs from local singers; he had already given series of lectures on folk songs in 1902 and 1903,[7] and like other young composers he was inspired by the example of Cecil Sharp in Somerset to go out into the field to search for them. Ralph's researches took him to Salisbury almshouses (Hussey's, or possibly Thomas Brown's in Castle St, and St Nicholas Hospital), the Alderbury union workhouse in Harnham, the Fox and Goose pub at Coombe Bissett (twice), and Stratford Toney.[8] Of the 18 songs he collected, including some that were well known or not 'true' folk songs, was one, 'An Acre of Land', [9] which in 1949, towards the end of his life, he included in a cantata for women's voices, *Folk Songs of the Four Seasons*.[10] He had heard it sung by Frank Bailey, an ex-soldier, in the Fox and Goose.[11]

A second consequence of the visits to Adeline's parents was that Ralph came to know and like the New Forest and its surroundings, to the extent that some of his early compositions depicted or were rooted in the area.[12] His first published work, in 1902, was his enduring setting of William Barnes's 'Linden Lea', which he misleadingly described on his title page as 'A Dorset Folk Song'.[13] In fact it is a dialect poem written by Barnes about his orchard at the Chantry in Mere.[14] More ambitious, but virtually unknown until its recent reconstruction and recording, is an extended orchestral work now issued as *Three Impressions for Orchestra*.[15] Two movements are inscribed 'Burley Heath' and 'The Solent', but the third brings us much closer to home. It is 'Harnham Down', and it was begun in July 1904,[16] so its inspiration was presumably the 1903 holiday and the folk-song collecting visit to Salisbury. It is a gentle, pastoral piece, about seven minutes long, whose slow, wistful melodies perfectly capture the mood of the prefacing quotation, from Matthew Arnold, which finishes: 'All the live murmur of a summer's day'.[17]

During the decade that followed this idyll Ralph became established as a leading English composer, living in London and Surrey, but wartime brought him back to Wiltshire. In 1914 he volunteered for the Royal Army Medical Corps and trained as a wagon orderly.[18] His unit spent the first half of 1916 at Sutton Veny in the Wylye valley where, during the previous year, more than a dozen timber hutted camps had been constructed, and a 'hutted hospital' for nearly 1,300 casualties was built, which opened during 1916.[19] His training, though it may have centred on the hospital and camp, presumably included

Ralph in military uniform, c1916 (BL MS Mus 1714/10/5, reproduced by kind permission of the Vaughan Williams Charitable Trust).

forays on to Salisbury Plain. If so, he doubtless recalled the folk song of that name which he had collected in Sussex in 1904,[20] and whose tale of a deserted lover and the gallows bears a certain resemblance to Hardy's Tess; we shall encounter her shortly.

From Sutton Veny Ralph's unit moved to active service in France in June 1916 and his subsequent war service did not bring him back to Wiltshire.[21] But during the 1920s he indulged in walking holidays, generally on the Wiltshire or Dorset chalklands, and on one of these in 1927 he had walked from Stapleford up on to Salisbury Plain (by the slow-coach road presumably) and was in Chitterne looking for a bed. At the cottage to which he was directed he encountered a fellow-soldier from RAMC days, and they sat up reminiscing about their army careers for most of the night.[22]

In 1924 he and Adeline had stayed in a friend's home at Oare, on the Marlborough Downs, and there he composed Flos Campi, the 'flower of the field', based on *The Song of Solomon*.[23] Some years later and now in his sixties, in 1938, he retreated to Wiltshire again to work, and stayed at Rose Cottage in Stapleford.[24] The work in question was his serene fifth symphony, and two new influences were uppermost in his mind. One, having just returned from receiving an award in Hamburg, was foreboding about Hitler's Germany and the course of world events. The other was a new found love, for Ursula Wood, who would eventually become his second wife. From Stapleford he wrote to her, 'I have been wonderful walks on the downs – they were perfect – sun, high wind and wonderful July field flowers – the kind I like best.' On one of these walks, he recounted to Ursula, he had ventured to Salisbury to see Walter Alcock, a distinguished composer in his own right and the cathedral organist, who was busy with his other passion, his model railway. He took Ralph into the dark empty cathedral and played Bach on the organ – an experience never to be forgotten.

One further influence which pervaded Ralph's life and drew him repeatedly to Wessex was his appreciation and fondness for the work of Thomas Hardy.[25] They never met, but in 1908 they had corresponded about setting a song from Hardy's *The Dynasts*, and around this period Ralph retraced part of Tess's journey on foot.[26] He was by no means the only composer to fall under Hardy's spell. His great friend Gustav Holst was driven with Hardy across Egdon Heath and composed what he regarded as his greatest work, his evocation of the opening of *Return of the Native*; Gerald Finzi, another close friend, set more than 50 of Hardy's poems, and Rutland Boughton based his opera *The Queen*

Ralph in 1952 (reproduced by kind permission of the Vaughan Williams Charitable Trust).

*of Cornwall* on a Hardy play.[27] Ralph's enthusiasm for Hardy did not result in any significant compositions until late in life. He was asked in 1950 to write incidental music for a radio adaptation of *The Mayor of Casterbridge*, and this resulted in a suite of four episodes (recently recorded) which includes a haunting 'Casterbridge' theme based on an old carol tune.[28] Then in 1954 he included a setting of the much-loved Hardy poem 'The Oxen' in his Christmas cantata *Hodie*.[29]

Detail of manuscript score of the Ninth Symphony, showing cancelled annotations to Wessex and Stonehenge (BL Add MS 50379-B, f2r, reproduced from Frogley, 2001, p39 with permission).

From Beethoven and Schubert onwards, ninth symphonies (often a composer's last) seem to have had a particular significance. Ralph began work on his ninth in 1956, and it was first performed a few months before his death in 1958. Initially his intention was to give it a title, 'A Salisbury Symphony' (thus bookending his orchestral symphonic output, which began with, 'A London Symphony' in 1914). The 'Salisbury' moniker did not stick, however. In his note for the first performance Ralph wrote (of the second movement, but it applies to the whole work) that it had started off with a programme, but '. . . it got lost on the journey – so now, oh no, we never mention it – and the music must be left to speak for itself – whatever that may mean'.[30] Nevertheless, the composer's numerous sketches and autograph scores survive, and are peppered with more than 50 verbal inscriptions heading or referring to specific passages, which were subsequently cancelled.[31] These, and the reminiscences of Michael Kennedy, friend and cataloguer of his music, that Ralph revealed a programme for the symphony which included Stonehenge, Salisbury Cathedral, and the 'ghostly drummer of Salisbury Plain', have enabled Vaughan Williams scholar Alain Frogley to reconstruct in considerable and plausible detail the topographical and literary themes which underlie the music.[32]

The symphony is in four movements. Although in the manuscript the first movement had been inscribed 'Wessex Prelude', the themes of this and the third movement cannot readily be linked to either the region or the novelist who coined its use. It is against the second and fourth movements that the inscriptions proliferate, and from these Frogley has uncovered their underlying programmes. The dramatic second movement, with its menacing opening, humming and bell-like effects – which puzzled critics at its early performances – portrays the final pages of *Tess of the d'Urbervilles*, in which she and Angel Clare find themselves benighted at Stonehenge, as they flee justice, and in the morning Tess is captured and after due process hanged for murder, as the Winchester clocks strike eight. Another Salisbury Plain context may be reflected in a persistent drumming theme, the Tidworth poltergeist or 'ghostly drummer'.

Discussion during rehearsals for the world premiere of the Ninth Symphony, St Pancras Town Hall, 1958 (BL MS Mus 1714/10/11, reproduced by kind permission of the Vaughan Williams Charitable Trust).

One motif in the final movement is inscribed in the manuscript '*Introibo in altare Dei*' ('I shall go in unto the altar of God'), from the Latin Vulgate translation of Psalm 42. Other indications in this movement refer to 'end of finale Salisbury' and 'steeple tune', from which Frogley deduces that the altar of God portrayed is intended to be Salisbury cathedral, and that the movement – and by extension the whole symphony – is a kind of pilgrimage through life which ends in this metaphor for one's spiritual destination. (One recalls that walk over the downs in 1938 to hear Bach played in the cathedral's cavernous darkness.[33]) But, as Frogley interprets the symphony, this is not the radiant progress of Bunyan's pilgrim – another pervading influence of Ralph's creative life, and one very much in his mind in 1938 – but a more agnostic, Hardyesque, journey, which takes the pilgrim to the altar of God in Salisbury, but also to the altar stone at Stonehenge, and to annihilation.

If the ninth symphony can be seen as the summation of the composer's lifelong devotion to Salisbury and its surroundings, there is also a fitting coda or epilogue.[34] After a first performance under Sir Malcolm Sargent in April 1958, the symphony was played again by Sargent at a promenade concert in early August, and Sir Adrian Boult was due to record it at the end of the month. Between the broadcast, which Ralph attended, and the recording sessions, Ralph and Ursula spent part of the intervening weeks on a touring holiday around Dorset, with their friend Gerald Finzi's widow, Joy, acting as chauffeuse.[35] Ursula, an accomplished writer and poet,[36] recalled with evident delight one of their expeditions:

> Joy drove us to Salisbury to see the cathedral floodlit. . . We stopped to see Old Sarum on the way, another view for Ralph over to Stonehenge and across the Plain. When we got to Salisbury we saw the cathedral transformed to gold, and details that one had not noticed standing out, so that the design of the whole was even more noble than in daylight. A dazzled owl flapped in and out of the lights gilding the spire and, as the evening got darker, both the blue night sky and the golden building intensified in brilliance.
>
> We had seen England in its most typical beauty of a cool, wet summer, with enough sunshine to ripen the corn, and to fill the hedges and road verges with Ralph's favourite wild flowers, late summer's profusion of yellow and white and lilac colours.

Ralph never went to the recording of his symphony. On the night before, 25/26 August 1958, he died in his sleep.

## Notes

1   Ordnance Survey 25-inch sheet Wilts 5.6 (1899 edn). The vicarage (now 'Pilgrims') was built in 1865, so was almost new: National Heritage List, no 1089934.

2   Connock, Stephen, 2000, 'Two Churchmen of Bemerton, Salisbury: Arthur Vaughan Williams (1860-1863)', *Journal of the RVW Society*, 17, 15; *VCH Wilts*, 6, 49.

3   Vaughan Williams, Ursula, 1964, *RVW: a biography of Ralph Vaughan Williams*, Oxford UP, 17.

4   *ibid*, 51. The priest who married them was the celebrated Revd W J Spooner.

5   *ibid*, 47; *The Times*, 26 Jan 1903.

6   Vaughan Williams, Ursula, *op cit*, 65.

7   Kendall, T, in L Foreman, ed, 1998, *Ralph Vaughan Williams in perspective*, Albion Press, 51-5.

8   Kennedy, Michael, 1996, *A catalogue of the works of Ralph Vaughan Williams*, 2nd ed,

Oxford UP, 254-5.

9 http://media.efdss.org.uk/resourcebank/docs/RB006AnAcreOfLand-KS2.pdf (accessed 23 Feb 2017)

10 Kennedy, Michael, *op cit*, 185-7. It was commissioned by the National Federation of Women's Institutes.

11 Perhaps Frank George Bailey, born about 1851, who was living in Britford in 1891, Standlynch in 1901 and Laverstock in 1911: Census returns.

12 Frogley, Alain, in A Frogley and A J Thomson, eds, 2013, *The Cambridge companion to Vaughan Williams*, Cambridge UP, 87, 103 n12.

13 Kennedy, Michael, *op cit,* 13. Around the same time he set another Barnes poem, 'Blackmwore by the Stour': Kennedy, *op cit,* 15.

14 Chedzoy, Alan, 1985, *William Barnes: a life of the Dorset poet*, Compton Press, 52.

15 It has been recorded by the Royal Liverpool Philharmonic Orchestra under Paul Daniel: *The Solent* (Albion Records, ALBCD016, 2013), tracks 1-3.

16 Kennedy, Michael, *op cit,* 23; discussion in Kuykendall, J B, 2015, 'Early orchestral works of Vaughan Williams recovered', *Notes*, 71, pt 3, 573-7. The score, edited by J F Brown, was published by Oxford UP in 2013. 'Harnham Down', incidentally, is not found on maps of the period, which always refer to 'Harnham Hill' (as now), but presumably the hill and the start of the drove road overlooking Salisbury is the intended location.

17 Kennedy, Michael, *op cit,* 23; the quotation is from *The Scholar Gypsy*, and Vaughan Williams returned to it in *An Oxford Elegy* (1949).

18 Vaughan Williams Ursula, *op cit,* 115-16.

19 *ibid*, 119-20; James, N D G, 1987, *Plain Soldiering*, Hobnob Press, 156-7, 200. Contrary to the impression given by biographies of Vaughan Williams, the camp was not on Salisbury Plain, but in the wooded Wylye valley.

20 Vaughan Williams, Ralph and Lloyd, A L, 1959, *The Penguin Book of English Folk Songs*, Penguin, 95.

21 Vaughan Williams, Ursula, *op cit,* 120, 123-32.

22 *ibid*, 167-8.

23 *ibid*, 155.

24 This para: Vaughan Williams, Ursula, *op cit,* 221-3; Cobbe, H, ed, 2008, *Letters of Ralph Vaughan Williams, 1895-1958*, Oxford UP, 263 (no 298); Neighbour, O, 2008, 'Ralph, Adeline, and Ursula Vaughan Williams: some facts and speculation', *Music and Letters* 89 (3), 337-45.

25 Frogley, Alain, 1986, 'Hardy in the music of Vaughan Williams', *Thomas Hardy Journal* 2 (3), 50-5; reprinted in *Journal of the RVW Society* 15 (June 1999), 8-9.

26 Vaughan Williams, Ursula, *op cit,* 84-5.

27 Chandler, John, 2009, *The Reflection in the Pond*, Hobnob Press, 198, 201-3.

28 Vaughan Williams, Ursula, *op cit,* 300; Kennedy, *op.cit,* 192, 214; *The Solent* (Albion Records, ALBCD016, 2013), tracks 12-15.

29 Kennedy, Michael, 1980, *The Works of Ralph Vaughan Williams,* 2nd ed, Oxford UP, 364, describes this as the high-point of the work.

30 Quoted in Frogley, Alain, 2001, *Vaughan Williams's Ninth Symphony*, Oxford UP, 256.

31 *ibid*, 258-9.

32 *ibid*, 256-94, from which the summary in the following two paragraphs is largely derived.

33  This connection is made by Neighbour, O, in Frogley, Alain, ed, 1996, *Vaughan Williams Studies*, Cambridge UP, 226-7; and by Day, J, 1998, *Vaughan Williams*, Oxford UP, 222

34  This paragraph and quotation: Vaughan Williams, Ursula, *op cit,* 398-9.

35  From 10 August (or earlier) until 18 August: Cobbe, *op cit*, 641 (nos 752-3).

36  Vaughan Williams, Ursula, 1996, *Collected poems*, Albion Music, 113-14; her poem 'Stonehenge' first published in 1959, uses musical analogies to describes the monument.

**Acknowledgements**

I am extremely grateful to Alain Frogley, Hugh Cobbe and Roy Bexon for their friendly assistance and advice, and to them and the British Library and Vaughan Williams Charitable Trust for permission to reproduce images.

Attributed to Edmund Rogers (1828-1878), View of Salisbury Cathedral tower and Spire. 1866-1869. Albumen print, carte de visite (Author's collection).

This carte de visite has no printed etiquette on the verso. It has 'E. Rogers The Close Salisbury' in manuscript on the verso. The dating of the photograph is based on the scaffolding on the top of the spire, which was part of the restoration campaign of 1866-1869.

# Women and Photography in 19th-century Salisbury[1]

## Anthony Hamber

In his article 'Images of Longespée: a personal view', published in *Sarum Chronicle* 15, David Richards makes a suggestion that Catherine Weed Ward (née Barnes) (1851-1913), an American photographer married to Henry Snowden Ward (1865-1911), editor of a number of British photographic periodicals, had been one of the earliest women commercial photographers in Britain, and that she may have been the first to have photographed the tomb of William Longespée on the South side of the Nave of Salisbury Cathedral.[2] The role of women in the early history of photography has been increasingly researched over the last three decades.[3] Previously, the received wisdom had been that the primary role of women in photography during the 19th century had been as assistants in the processing and printing of photographs. Few had been 'camera operators', ie had actually taken photographs. Similarly there had been very few women professional photographers. This view has long been due a complete overhaul. A current web site dedicated to Women Photographers in 19th Century Britain lists more than 160 who operated commercially during the 19th century.[4] This number will continue to rise as further research takes place.

English women photographers of the 19th century primarily fell into two camps. Firstly, there were those who were amateurs. These were predominantly from well off families – given the cost of equipment and materials – and had an aptitude and appetite to master complex chemistry and optics, and a willingness to get their hands dirty. They might come from families – or have husbands – who were actively involved in practical science, and/or photography.

The other camp was populated by the commercially driven. Some of these were entrepreneurs wishing to exploit the new market opportunities. Others were forced by circumstance to look for new forms of income.

Women were actively involved in the taking of photographs from the very dawn of photography. In England, Constance Talbot (née Mundy, 1811-1880), the wife of one of the inventors of photography, William Henry Fox Talbot (1800-77), was taking photographs in 1839.

An example of an early woman photographer was Sarah Anne Bright (1793-1866), daughter of Richard Bright, Sr (1754-1840), a merchant and banker, and also a keen amateur man of science. He had worked closely with leading scientists such as Joseph Priestley and Humphry Davy and had met Benjamin Franklin in Paris. Bright set up a chemical laboratory at his home, Ham Green House, near Pill, overlooking the River Avon, some seven miles downstream from Bristol. Professor Larry Schaaf has now identified that Sarah Anne Bright probably made one of the earliest photographs as early as the summer of 1839 at the family home, Ham Green House.[5]

There were professional women photographers active in Great Britain before Catherine Weed Ward was born. Perhaps the very first was Ann Cooke (b1796), who set up a Daguerreotype studio in Lincoln in 1844. Another was Jane Nina Wigley (1820-1883) who opened a Daguerreotype studio in Newcastle on 22nd September 1845. She then moved to London in 1848 and set up a studio in the Kings Road, Chelsea before moving to Fleet Street.[6] Wigley was apparently a pioneer in the use of a prism in the camera in order to reverse the Daguerreotype image. However, in 1850, Jane Wigley received some significant criticism from Thomas Malone, who with Nicolaas Henneman ran one of the leading London photographic studios, a studio financially supported by Fox Talbot. In a letter to Talbot, Malone wrote that cheap licences to practise the Daguerreotype 'will not add to the dignity of the Art' and Richard Beard, another leading London photographer and the holder of the right to issue Daguerreotype licenses in England, regretted giving a licence to a Miss Wigley. 'The badness of her pictures & the absurdity of her advertisements tends to bring the Daguerreotype into disrepute'.[7]

In 1849, Arnold Ruge (1802-80), the German philosopher and political writer and association of Karl Marx (1818-80) had become a political refugee in London. The following year Marx wrote to Frederick Engels (1820-95) that Ruge 'whose finances seem to be in extreme disarray, intended to buy a Daguerreotype establishment and to travel the country as a Daguerreotype photographer'.[8]

By September 1850 Ruge was resident in Brighton. There, he and his wife Agnes bought a photographic studio from a Frenchman, Captain Becquet, and set up as a professional photographer in Brighton. The Daguerreotype was the process used, which was of course expensive due to the requirement for silver to coat the metal plates. Agnes encountered trouble with the drying process via a flame – the plates ending up with a brown strip through the centre of the photo. Arnold Ruge was in charge at first, but the processes were fiddly and better suited to female fingers, so Agnes took over. While the Ruge studio was still active in 1854, Agnes noted that 'soon afterwards photographers popped up everywhere', and 'we found giving [language] lessons more pleasant and more lucrative', so they sold their apparatus to 'Mr Wappett'. The Ruges lost at least £50 on the 'whole undertaking'.[9]

The number of women photographers increased during the 1850s and this was in part due to formal training. In 1853, the London-based photographer Nicolaas Henneman (1813-1898) offered Ladies classes in photography costing three guineas, including one private lesson.

These classes took place in the Royal Panopticon of Science and Art located on London's Leicester Square.[10] By the 1860s, some women photographers were securing significant roles in public sector organisations, such as Isabel Agnes Cowper (1826?-1911), who became the photographer at the South Kensington Museum – now the Victoria & Albert Museum – in 1868.[11] The 1861 Census for England, Wales & Scotland listed 204 women working professionally in photographic businesses.

The first women professional photographer in Salisbury appears to have been Mary Ann Rogers (c1828-1911), wife of Edmund Rogers, also referred to as Marianne Rogers. Mary Ann Bolland had been born in Oxford in 1828. A school mistress, she married Edmund on 2nd January 1851 in Gillingham, Dorset and they set up home in Britford. The 1861 census found Edmund living in Britford with Mary Ann and three children, sons Edmund (aged 9) and William (6) and a daughter, Emma (1). He was a wood and general turner and she was a school mistress.

Edmund was born in Salisbury in 1828. The 1841 census found him living with his parents in New Street. His father, William, was a fruiterer/greengrocer. The 1851 census lists him as an ivory and wood turner.

Having taught himself photography (probably from a published manual accompanied by practical experimentation), Edmund set up as a photographer in East Harnham by at least February of 1862, though advertisements in the late 1850s indicated that he also had an address in the High Street from which he ran his wood turning business. However, Rogers seems to have had at least one side line, that of selling English and Belgian canaries and a few mules![12]

The early 1860s was a boom time for photography in Great Britain and clearly Edmund had identified the opportunity and somehow acquired the necessary knowledge, associated craft skills and financial wherewithal to set up in business. By February 1863 Edmund's photographic business appears to have been prospering, since he advertised his turning lathe for sale.[13]

*left:* Edmund Rogers (1828-1878), Full-length portrait of a woman. 1862-1864. Albumen print, carte de visite (Author's collection).
*right:* Verso of same. This etiquette refers to Rogers's first studio (Author's collection)

In 1864 he moved his studio to the Corner House in De Vaux Place. This may have been a result of business being slow in East Harnham and appreciation that in order to be commercially successful he needed to operate a studio closer to the city centre. The residents of the Close might also provide useful customers and encourage their guests and visitors to attend Corner House.

Edmund Rogers seems, like many early photographers, to have concentrated on portraiture though he – and probably his wife – exploited the commercial demands for topographic and architectural views as they increased from the late 1850s. One can note from an examination of the verso of cartes de visite from the Rogers studio changes to the *etiquette* – the advertisement of the photographic studio. One particularly noticeable element is that there was a move from 'E. Rogers' to just 'Rogers', which may indicate that Mary Ann was also acting as a photographer.

One of the facets of the rapid development of the commercial photographic market during the 1850s and 1860s was the introduction of a number of

*left:* Anonymous photographer. View of the façade of Salisbury Cathedral taken before 1865. Albumen print, carte de Visite (Author's collection)
*right:* Edmund or Mary Ann Rogers. View of the St. Ann Street Gate from Exeter Street. 1860s. Albumen print, carte de visite (Author's collection)

Verso of three carte de visite photographs from the Rogers studio. 1860s and 1870s. (Author's collection). While the left and centre cards refer to "Rogers", the card on the right specifically refers to Edmund Rogers.

photographic formats. These included, in terms of chronological introduction, the stereoscopic view, the carte de visite and the Cabinet formats. The stereoscopic view (dimensions of around 8 x 17cms) became popular from the early 1850s, even though it required a specialist viewer. The carte de visite format (dimensions of around 6 x 10cms) was patented in Paris, by photographer André Adolphe Eugène Disdéri (1819-89) in 1854 and became popular from the early 1860s. The Cabinet view (dimensions of around 16.5 x 11cms) was introduced in 1868 and widely used for photographic portraiture and architectural views after 1870.[14]

James Wesley Miell (1837-1901). General View of Salisbury Cathedral. c1875. Albumen print, Cabinet card (Author's Collection). This Cabinet card is unusual in that it represents an early form of Christmas greeting card.

Carte de visite 'Cartomania' rose rapidly from around 1859 and many millions were sold during the 1860s. As the SJ reported in February 1862, 'It is a curious fact that the cartes de visite have for the present superseded all other sized photographic portraits. This is rather singular, inasmuch as we did not adopt it until it had been popular in Paris for three years'.[15] Edmund Rogers was quick to exploit this format for portraiture and stuck with it as his primary format, a fact that he underlined from his early advertisements in the spring of 1862. While the majority of portraits would have been private commissions of the inhabitants of Salisbury, some were more formal. In February 1866 it was

William Russell Sedgefield (1826-1901). Salisbury Cathedral, The West Door. *c*1860. No.382 from the series Sedgefield's English Scenery. Albumen prints, Stereoscopic view (Author's collection).

noted that Rogers had taken a group portrait of 12 cathedral choristers, which he had published in a carte de visite format.[16] Edmund also photographed local dignitaries, such as the Bishop of Salisbury, Walter Hamilton (1808-1869), his wife and daughter. He registered these for copyright.[17] Rogers published carte de visite and Cabinet format photographs which could be obtained either directly from him or through the bookseller and stationer, Frederick Augustus Blake, in the Market Place.[18]

In the autumn of 1867, Frederick Treble (*c*1830-1915), who had set up a photographic studio in Catherine Street in 1862 and in 1865 took a three year lease out on a premises in the High Street, decided to leave Salisbury. Rogers advertised in December 1867 that since Treble was selling his negatives, he would be happy to print copies from the same. It is likely that Mary Ann would have helped with the printing of these negatives. [19]

In July 1868 Mary Ann advertised that she wished to open a school at their home in July 1868.[20] Whether this reflected Edmund's business falling on harder times as a result of the economic recession between 1867 and 1869, brought about by the impact on exports due to the American recession post-civil war, is unclear. In addition there was increasing competition from some ten other commercial photographers in Salisbury. However, the Rogers' school was still operating at the time of Mary Ann's death.

The 1871 census provides the following information about Edmund and Mary Ann from the Harnham Bridge Road District 4 Salisbury who were living in De Vaux Place.

| Edmund Rogers | Head | 43 | Photographer | b Salisbury |
|---|---|---|---|---|
| Mariannie [*sic*] Rogers | Wife | 43 | Photographer wife | b Oxfordshire |
| Edith Rogers | daughter | 9 | | b East Harnham |
| Charles Rogers | son | 7 | | b East Harnham |
| Florence M Rogers | daughter | 6 | | b Salisbury |
| Annie Rogers | daughter | 4 | | b Salisbury |

It is likely that Mary Ann Rogers had assisted her husband in running his photographic business during the 1860s, perhaps also taking photographs. Yet it remains significant that she gave her profession as a 'photographer' in the 1871 census, indicating that she took photographs, rather than had a role in processing and printing the negatives taken by her husband. However, quite when Mary Ann started taking photographs has yet to be established.

Edmund died in 1878. Mary Ann appears in the 1881 census, still listing her profession as 'photographer'. She was also listed as a professional photographer in the Kelly's 1880 and 1889 directories for Hampshire, Wiltshire and Dorset.

Mary Ann was a visitor in the Southampton suburb of Millbrook in the 1891 census, still listed as a photographer. The 1901 census recorded Mary Ann, aged 73, still living in De Vaux Place, though she seems to have retired. Her profession was recorded as managing 'let apartments', together with one of her daughters, Edith. A decade later the 1911 census recorded she was still living in De Vaux Place with her three spinster daughters who were running a school in the house. No profession is recorded for Mary Ann who is simply described as a widow. Mary Ann died in the same year.

Having established that there were over 160 professional women photographers active in 19th century Britain, and that Salisbury had a woman professional photographer a generation before Catherine Weed Ward visited Salisbury to photograph the Longespée tomb, one may examine the suggestion that she was the first to photograph the Longespée tomb.

Again one should distinguish between amateur and professional photographers who documented the Cathedral and, specifically, their activities inside Salisbury Cathedral. Early professional photographers such as Russell Sedgfield (1826-1902), who photographed the Cathedral in 1853, and Roger Fenton (1819-1869), who photographed the Cathedral in 1858, either took external general views, or a limited number of general views of the interior.

Several other photographers documented the cathedral and exhibited these images at major exhibitions. This was part of a wider rise in interest in Gothic architecture, in part due to the Gothic Revival inspired by the work of Augustus Welby Northmore Pugin (1812-52) who moved to Salisbury with his wife in 1834 and in the following year bought half an acre of land, at

Alderbury, on which he built a medieval-inspired house for his family, called 'St Marie's Grange'. The Pugin family left Salisbury in 1837 and the house remained empty until sold in 1841.

George Charles Warren (1828-1901), a London photographer working for Mawson (see 'A Faithful Likeness' p95) exhibited photographs of the 'Interior of Chapter House, Salisbury Cathedral' (cat 450), 'Arch Details from Winchester and Salisbury Cathedrals' (cat 457), 'Salisbury Cathedral' (cat 579) and 'Architectural View of West Front, Salisbury Cathedral' (cat 835) at the 1854 Photographic Society Exhibition. Warren also exhibited views of monuments by the English Neo-classical sculptor John Flaxman (1755-1826).

In 1858, Archibald Lewis Cocke (1824-1896), a London photographer who with his brother managed a Daguerreotype studio between 1847 and 1850 before branching off on his own, exhibited some eleven of his photographs of Salisbury at that year's Architectural Photographic Association exhibition. None were interior views of the Cathedral.

Many Stereo photographic views of the Cathedral and some of its monuments were available from around 1860 onwards. One such example is a stereo photograph by Russell Sedgfield of the tomb of Bishop Giles de Bridport (died 1262). By at least 1874 Brown & Co. of the Canal advertised a 10 x 12 inch photograph of the Giles de Bridport tomb costing 3s 6d unmounted and 4s 6d mounted.

The Longespée tomb posed a significant challenge to early photographers since the effigy required scaffolding or a complex mirror arrangement in

William Russell Sedgefield (1826-1901). Tomb of Bishop Bridport, Salisbury Cathedral. c1860. No 391 from the series Sedgefield's English Scenery. Albumen prints, Stereoscopic view (Author's collection).

order to create a full-frontal, full-length photograph that mirrored the view depicted in the painting by the English architectural draughtsman, engraver, illuminator, and antiquary Henry Shaw (1800-1873) reproduced in his *Dresses and Decorations of the Middle Ages from the Seventh to the Seventeenth Centuries* first published by William Pickering in 1843, and later by Henry G. Bohn in 1858. As will be seen below, side views of similar tombs in the cathedral posed fewer problems.

While photographic historians have tended to focus on the application of the carte de visite to portraiture, it was also extensively used to document architecture and sculpture. Local photographers would provide sets of carte de visite images of Gothic Cathedrals and new Neo-Gothic churches together with their fixtures and fittings. For instance a significant set of carte de visite photographs of St Peter's Bournemouth'– built in a number of phases between 1844 and 1879 - were taken by a local photographer William Wyatt Burnand of Longfleet, Poole. These included views of the pulpit, lectures and font, and were sold through local retailers such as Alfred Brook, a 'Fine Art & Fancy Goods Repository' in Poole. In 1861 Burnand had his own business as a chemist in Old Orchard, Poole, Dorset. By 1871 he had moved to New Town Terrace, High Street, Longfleet, Poole, where he operated as a photographer until at least 1901. He died at Guildford in 1909.

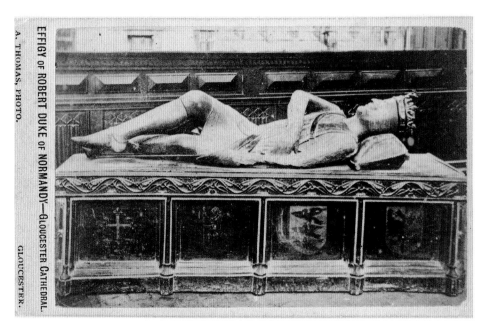

Abraham Thomas. Effigy of Robert Duke of Normandy – Gloucester Cathedral. *c*1870. Albumen print, carte de visite (Author's collection).

A carte de visite photograph of the tomb of Robert Curthose, Duke of Normandy (*c*1051-1134) in Gloucester Cathedral photographed by Abraham Thomas of Gloucester – and dating to *c*1870 - provides evidence to suggest that there could well have been similar photographs of the Longespée tomb.[21]

The Curthose tomb was carved *c*1260, slightly later than the date of *c*1240 attributed to the Longespée tomb.[22] While the Curthose tomb posed similar technical challenges to photographers in terms of taking a full-frontal, full-length photograph, Thomas decided to record a side view.

In conclusion it may be assumed that it was likely that the tomb of William Longespée had been photographed before the campaign undertaken by Catherine Weed Ward though whether Mary Ann Rogers had photographed the tomb remains to be established. However, the author continues to search for either a reference to such a photograph or an extant example.

## Notes

1 This article is based on a wider research project on the history of photography in Salisbury from 1839 to 1880.

2 Richards David, 'Images of Longespée: a personal view', *Sarum Chronicle*, 15, 99-108. The photograph was reproduced in Gleeson White, *The Cathedral Church of Salisbury*, 1898.

3 An early article was published by Heathcote & Pauline F. Heathcote 'The feminine influence: Aspects of the role of women in the evolution of photography in the British Isles', History of Photography, 1988 259-73. This was followed by Bernard Heathcote and Pauline Heathcote, *A Faithful Likeness – The First Photographic Portrait Studios in the British Isles 1841-1855*, Bernard and Pauline Heathcote, Lowdham, 2002. See also Keith Adamson, 'Early Provincial Studios', *The Photographic Journal*, February, 1987 74-78; Keith Adamson, 'More Early Studios' [Part 1], *The Photographic Journal*, January, 1988 32-36; Keith Adamson, 'More Early Studios' [Part 2], *The Photographic Journal*, July, 1988 305–309.

4 See https://womenphotographers.wordpress.com/

5 See http://foxtalbot.bodleian.ox.ac.uk/tempestuous-teacups-and-enigmatic-leaves/

6 See Database of 19th Century Photographers and Allied Trades in London 1841-1901 http://www.photolondon.org.uk/pages/details.asp?pid=8431

7 Letter from Thomas Malone to William Henry Fox Talbot dated 15th February, 1850. See http://foxtalbot.dmu.ac.uk/

8 *Karl Marx Frederick Engels Collected Works*, Volume 38 1844-1851, International Publishers, New York, 1983 342-343.

9 I thank Rosemary Ashton for providing this information from the copy of the Agnes Ruge memoir in her possession. This copy was provided to Rosemary Ashton by Arnold Ruge, the great-grandson of Arnold Ruge. See Rosemary Ashton, *Little Germany: Exile and Asylum in Victorian England*, Oxford University Press, 1986 140.

10 Advertisement in the *Art-Journal Advertiser*, September, 1853 lxxxii. Henneman was

the former manservant of William Henry Fox Talbot. Supported financially by Talbot, Henneman had set up a photographic business at 122 Regent Street, London in 1847.

11  See http://www.vam.ac.uk/blog/factory-presents/international-womens-day-historic-women-va

12  *SJ*, Saturday 8th February 1862 5 and 15th February 5.

13  *SJ*, Saturday 21 February 1863.4.

14  The stereoscopic view was made up from two images taken from slightly different positions, mimicking the distance between human eyes, each 76 x 75 cm (3 x 3 in) mounted on a card 178 x 83 mm (7 in x 3.25 in). The carte de visite was a card sized 64 x 100 mm (2.5 x 4 in). The Cabinet photograph was mounted on a card typically measuring 108 x 165 mm (4 $\frac{1}{4}$ x 6 $\frac{1}{2}$ in.)

15  *SJ*, Saturday 1st February 1862 7. An article republished from *Once a Week*, 25th January, 1862 134-137.

16  *SJ*, Saturday 3rd February, 1866 8. Rogers registered a photograph of 'Group of the choristers of Salisbury Cathedral' in May 1867. *British Journal of Photography*, 31st May 1867 262.

17  'Two portraits of Mrs Walter Kerr Hamilton and Miss Constance Hamilton' were noted by the *British Journal of Photography*, 1st February 1867 58. 'Group of the choristers of Salisbury Cathedral' (BJP, 31st May 1867 262)

18  *SJ*, Saturday 21st August 1869 4.

19  *SJ*, Saturday 14th December 1867 4.

20  *SJ*, Saturday 18th July 1868 5.

21  Abraham Thomas was operating as a commercial photographer in Gloucester by at least 1868, and his carte de visite of the Richard Curthose tomb dates to around the 1860s or early 1870s.

22  See Rachel Dressler, 'Cross-legged Knights and signification in English Medieval Tomb Sculpture', *Studies in Iconography* Vol. 21 (2000), 91-121.

# What's in a Nameplate?

## Philip Rabbetts and Joe Newman

The inspiration for this article came from a phone call to Philip as local contact for Wiltshire Family History Society. Robert Speare is a railway researcher interested in the locomotives introduced towards the end of the Second World War by the Southern Railway which were named after towns and villages in the West Country. The Company made a point of holding a ceremony as each locomotive was introduced and named. The local dignitary who officiated was given a coffee table with a suitable inscription, and Robert had set himself the task of tracing what happened to these. Could the Salisbury branch of Wiltshire Family History Society help him, with particular reference to the engine named *Salisbury*?

Usually family historians work backwards in time, from one generation to the previous one. This exercise presented something of a challenge, to go forwards in time by more than 70 years. A visit to the Guildhall quickly established that the Mayor in July 1945 was Alfred Courtney who was a popular and energetic Mayor, perhaps worthy of further study.

We found that his two daughters had married service-men from the USA and Canada, so we concentrated on a surviving son and his descendants. As a result, Robert was able to trace the present owner of the coffee table given to the Mayor of Salisbury and he has determined what happened to the majority of the 26 coffee tables which were produced. Happily, the *Salisbury* table has survived, though in common with many there is some fading of the paint colours.

As one of the original *Salisbury* nameplates belongs to Salisbury Museum Joe was asked if he could trace the locomotive's history, particularly as 2017 marks 50 years since steam trains ran regularly through Salisbury.

In the summer of 1967, the use of steam hauled trains on British Railways Southern Region was drawing to a close as preparations were made for the change to diesel and electric traction. On Saturday 8 July 1967, the last steam hauled services ran to and from Salisbury.[1] As a result of these changes, large numbers of redundant steam engines were dispersed around the depots of southern England. Over the coming months they were scheduled to be taken to South Wales to be cut up for scrap. During this transition, many locomotives, *en route* to Wales, were hauled to the Salisbury shed which became renowned as a resting place for engines awaiting their final call.

On Saturday 19 August 1967, a row of rusting, dilapidated locomotives stood impotently alongside Churchfields Road, Salisbury. Opposite Stephenson Road was one which carried the number 34002.[2] Its coupling and connecting rods had been removed, it was dirty and careworn, and on the side of the boiler casing could be seen the outline where once a nameplate had been fixed. An enthusiast had chalked the characters '21C002'[3] along the front above the buffer beam, while on the smokebox door was drawn a semi-circle containing the word 'SOUTHERN'. These additions were a reminder of the first time the locomotive had visited Salisbury on Monday 9 July 1945.

The locomotive 34002 in a dilapidated condition on Salisbury shed adjacent to Stephenson Road, 19 August 1967. © David Mant

At that time there was beginning to be an air of optimism for the future. The conflict with Germany was over and that with Japan was clearly drawing to a close. Although Britain's railways were very run down as a result of the requirements of the war effort, there were new developments as the companies began to plan for a return to more normal operations. For the Southern Railway, one goal was the reintroduction of trains from London to its holiday destinations along the coast of North Devon and North Cornwall from Ilfracombe to Padstow.

Trains such as the Atlantic Coast Express, one of the company's most prestigious services, were hauled between Waterloo and Exeter by the most powerful and heaviest of the railway's locomotives. Beyond Exeter, such engines were prohibited from crossing Meldon Viaduct on Dartmoor, and from using the more lightly constructed branch lines to the coast. In order to allow for the introduction of heavier trains to the far Southwest in post-war Britain, the Southern Railway began, in mid-December 1944, to build new Pacific locomotives.[4] Designed by the company's Chief Mechanical Engineer, Mr O V S Bulleid, these engines were a smaller version of his *Merchant Navy* class which had been introduced in 1941[5] and were in use on the heaviest trains between Waterloo and Exeter. The new locomotives were designed to meet the load limitations on bridges and tracks west of Exeter and to be as light as possible, while being able to haul heavy passenger and freight trains.

They were to be named after towns, villages, and other locations in Wiltshire, Dorset, Devon and Cornwall that were served by the Southern Railway and the class of locomotive was appropriately called the *West Country* class.[6]

Like their predecessors the *West Country* class engines had some innovative mechanical features and were equipped with superb boilers which generated copious quantities of steam. They also had a striking appearance with the 'air-smoothed' casing which covered the boiler giving rise to the nickname 'Spam Cans'. Painted in malachite green with three yellow horizontal stripes along the boiler casing, they presented a definite contrast to the black locomotive livery used in war-time. On the smokebox door was a circular brass plate bearing the word 'SOUTHERN'.

The locomotive 21C102 Salisbury when first completed – official Southern Railway photo © National Railway Museum/Science and Society Picture Library

Alfred Courtney in the cab of 21C102 on 9 July 1945 with driver, C Wakem, 33 Nursery Road, Salisbury, and fireman Mr Kiddle of 1, Hartington Road, Salisbury. © National Railway Museum/ Science and Society Picture Library

The first three *West Country* engines were completed at Brighton locomotive works in May and June 1945.[7] The sequence of names was *Exeter, Salisbury,* and *Plymouth,*[8] and they were to be numbered 21C101, 21C102, and 21C103 respectively.[9] This numbering, which was unusual in Great Britain, was a variation of the system used on the Continent.[10] All three locomotives were allocated to Exmouth Junction depot at Exeter for use in Devon and Cornwall.[11]

For locomotive 21C102 there was a naming ceremony in Salisbury on Monday 9 July 1945 attended by senior management from the Southern Railway, including Lord Radnor who was Deputy Chairman, the designer Mr O V S Bulleid, and various councillors and officials from Salisbury. The Mayor, Alfred Courtney, officiated with *Salisbury* being the first of its class to be named.[12] Both the Chairman of the Southern Railway and the Mayor referred to the great part the railways had played in supporting the recent D-Day campaign. Later in the week there were similar ceremonies in Exeter and Plymouth to name their

engines.[13] In each case, the leading local dignitary was given a photograph of the engine, signed by the directors of the Southern Railway, and a small coffee table with an attached inscribed silver plate marking the occasion. The table top was decorated with the same coat of arms displayed on the enamelled crest attached to each side of the locomotive.

The coffee table presented to the Mayor. Private collection.

Alfred Courtney was born near Salisbury in 1885, served in the Royal Navy from 1900 to 1920, tried to start a business in Birkenhead, but returned to Salisbury, running a furnishing business and then a fish and chip shop. He was elected to the City Council as a representative of St Edmund's Ward in 1930.

There were some rather patronising reports in the press in 1939[14] that he had been elected Mayor in spite of his humble background but he had to wait until the end of the war before he could take up office. He was popular and served during the peace celebrations. He would support worthy causes by practical efforts to raise money, going out into the streets with a barrel organ and collecting box. His family recalls that he had a particular interest in Eventide homes. He continued to serve on the Council until 1954 and died in 1958.[15]

After the naming ceremony *Salisbury* travelled to Exeter to be put directly into service. On Tuesday 10 July 1945 it was recorded as being the first of the *West Country* locomotives to reach Ilfracombe, on the 1.40 pm from Exeter. On the return journey, it was photographed at Braunton by Mr H D Fuller.[16]

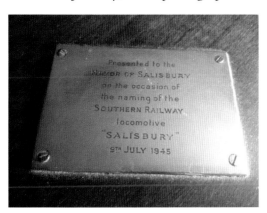

The inscribed silver plaque on the coffee table. Private collection.

For the next 19 years, *Salisbury* was used primarily in Devon and Cornwall as intended. Renumbered 34002 by British Railways in January 1949[17] it would have visited Salisbury; but it was never allocated to the locomotive depot there.[18] In September 1964, it was transferred to Eastleigh and was used for a time as a stationary boiler, supplying steam to the railway workshops.[19] The locomotive was finally transferred to Nine Elms depot, Battersea in January 1965,[20] being withdrawn from service there in April 1967.[21] On Sunday 9 July, 1967 *Salisbury* was photographed out of use at Nine Elms.[22] By this time the front number plate and the two nameplates had been removed – they were already collectors' items - and, like so many redundant steam locomotives, *Salisbury* stood sadly awaiting its fate.

Its last run, from Salisbury via Bath to Gloucester and on to South Wales, was not without incident, a mechanical fault leading to it needing repairs in Gloucester shed. While there, *Salisbury* was cleaned and partly repainted by enthusiasts who also added the legend 'The Pride of Gloucester'[23] to its tender

The preserved nameplate of Salisbury on display in the Railway Social Club. Photo by Roy Bexon with kind permission of Salisbury Museum ©

before it was towed on its final journey to Newport on Sunday 24 September.[24] It was cut up at Cashmore's scrapyard in October 1967,[25] having covered in excess of one million miles in a service life of 22 years.[26]

Despite the engine being broken up, one of the nameplates has returned to Salisbury. When locomotives were scrapped, the city after which they were named was offered one of the nameplates and shields, the others being sold. Thus, the nameplate of *Salisbury* was given by British Railways to the City of New Sarum. The Council decided on 6 January 1969 that the nameplate should be offered to Salisbury Museum in St Ann Street. It was then agreed that, due to lack of space, the nameplate could go on display in the Railway Social Club's premises in Fisherton Street when the buildings were ready later in the year, provided that certain security measures were put in place. The nameplate was loaned to The Social Club on 28 January 1970 on the understanding that it would be returned to Salisbury Museum when it moved to larger premises and there was space to display it.[27]

The nameplate consists of three parts which are of cast gunmetal. At the top is the name 'SALISBURY' and at the bottom a smaller plate identifying the engine as belonging to the 'West Country Class'. In between, set in a shield, is an enamel plaque containing a replica of the coat of arms of the City, identical to the one given to the Mayor.

In 2012 the nameplate was placed in the Railway Social Club's new premises in the ex-Great Western Railway station, designed by I K Brunel.[28] Thus a memento of a locomotive designed by one innovative engineer rests in a building designed by another.

## Acknowledgments

Thanks are due to: Robert Speare for the initial enquiry and advice; colleagues in WFHS for their help; descendants of Alfred Courtney for their assistance; David Mant for information about and photograph of the locomotive's last visit to Salisbury; Valerie Goodrich of Salisbury Museum for her help.

## Notes

1   Nicholas, John and Reeve, George, 2004, *Main Line to the West part 1*, Irwell Press, 202

2   Mant, David, private communication (received 16 March 2017)

3   The enthusiast was in error - it should have read '21C102' – see reference 9

4   Steam locomotives with certain types of wheel arrangement came to be known by special names. One that was commonly used in Great Britain was 'Pacific' or 4-6-2 where there are four leading wheels on two axles, six powered and coupled driving wheels on three axles, and two trailing wheels on one axle. See Simmons, Jack and Biddle, Gordon, 1997, *The Oxford Companion to British Railway History*, 562.

5   *Railway Magazine* 1941, Vol. 87, 173

6   *Southern Railway Magazine* 1945, vol. XXIII, no. 245,124

7   Bradley D L, 1976, *Locomotives of the Southern Railway part 2*, The Railway Correspondence and Travel Society, 57

8   Bradley D L, 1976, *Locomotives of the Southern Railway part 2*, The Railway Correspondence and Travel Society, 56

9   *The Railway Magazine* 1945, vol. 91,302

10  In this style of numbering, the letter 'C' indicates that there are three pairs of coupled wheels; the first number, '2', represents the two carrying axles of the front bogie and the second number,'1', the carrying axle under the cab. The number '101' begins the sequence of individual numbers of the engines.

11  From Southern E-Group data at http://www.semgonline.com/steam/blp_dat.html (accessed 8 March 2017)

12  *Salisbury Times* 13 July 1945 and *Salisbury & Winchester Journal* 13 July 1945

13  *Southern Railway Magazine* 1945, vol. XXIII, no. 245,125

14  *Daily Herald* 4 July 1939. Reports also appeared in the *Birmingham Gazette* 5 October 1939 and *Wiltshire Times* 8 July 1939.

15  *Salisbury Journal* 26 September 1958 and *Salisbury Times & South Wiltshire Gazette* 26 September 1958

16  Fuller H D, in *The Railway Magazine* 1945,vol. 91,302-303

17  Bradley D L, 1976, *Locomotives of the Southern Railway part 2*, The Railway Correspondence and Travel Society, 105

18  From Southern E-Group data at http://www.semgonline.com/steam/blp_dat.html

(accessed 8 March 2017)

19 Pigott, Nick, in *The Railway Magazine* 2011, vol. 157, 49

20 From BR Data Base at http://www.brdatabase.info/sites.php?page=depots&subpage= locos&id=382 (accessed 13 March 2017)

21 From BR Data Base at http://www.brdatabase.info/locoqry.php?action=locodata&id =346201002&type=S&loco=34002 (accessed 22 February 2017)

22 Catlin, Geoff, 2011, in *Nine Elms, Sunday 9th July 1967, The Final Day* http://svsfilm. com/nineelms/catlin.htm (accessed 15 February 2017)

23 Norman Preedy photograph in http://railphotoprints.uk/p978695097/ h549D501C#h5be5b1bc (accessed 30 March 2017)

24 Berry, Pete, 2014, in *Trainspotting Season,* National Railway Museum http://www. nrm.org.uk/NRM/PlanaVisit/Events/trainspotting/stories (accessed 15 February 2017)

25 From Bulleid Society data at http://www.bulleidsociety.org/OVS_Bulleid/OVSB_ Light_Pacifics.html (accessed 22 February 2017)

26 Bradley D L, 1976, *Locomotives of the Southern Railway part 2*, The Railway Correspondence and Travel Society, 108

27 Salisbury Museum accession no. SBYWM:1969.32

28 MacDermot E T, *History of the Great Western Railway* 1964, Vol. 1, 213

# Pilgrimage in Medieval Salisbury

## David Richards

In pre-Reformation England pilgrims visited holy places and saintly shrines for the betterment of their souls in the life hereafter and for the improvement of their physical health during their own lifetime. Salisbury pilgrims can be looked at in three groups: firstly, those who came specifically for St Osmund, Our Lady of Salisbury and the relics and holy images of the cathedral; secondly those Salisbury folk who left the city to visit shrines elsewhere in England and Europe; and thirdly pilgrims who passed through Salisbury, because of its geographical location, on their way to other shrines. Pilgrimage in Salisbury will be examined through the lenses of the cathedral's archive of indulgences, Salisbury Museum's collection of pilgrim badges[1] and the 1536 inventory of the cathedral's treasures.[2] The inhabitants of late 15th century Salisbury were taught by the church that there were two forms of sin: mortal or grave (which cut the sinner off from God) and venial or minor. The church granted forgiveness to sinners who truly repented. The consequences of sin were vividly displayed in the Doom Painting in Salisbury's St Thomas's Church in a visually

St James of Compostela, St Thomas's Church, Salisbury

pragmatic image accessible and understandable to all, even to those who could not speak or read Latin. The painting showed Christ on the Day of Judgement separating 'the sheep from the goats',[3] with the blessed, absolved, repentant sinners on the right hand of Christ being guided up to the sunlit, celestial city of heaven by a pope. This was contrasted with the cursed, unrepentant, unforgiven sinners on the left hand of Christ being dragged by a devil down into the fires of hell. However, the painting fails to explain the medieval church's teaching that all sin contaminates or 'stains' the sinner and that this must be cleansed and purified, over a period of time, in purgatory after death, before it was possible to enter into heaven. This cleansing time could be reduced during the sinner's lifetime by good works, donations to the church, indulgences and pilgrimage.[4] The majority of indulgences were partial, being measured in days although there were plenary indulgences[5] that cancelled punishment of sin in purgatory. Indulgences have been described as pardons or even as passports to paradise.[6]

## Indulgences in Salisbury

Salisbury Cathedral Archives have a collection of 60 indulgences[7] or pardons, hand written in Latin on vellum. Indulgences were issued by popes, archbishops and bishops as members of the church that was God's agent on earth. Many indulgences were granted to help with building or repairing churches, some for attending a saint's festival and others for praying for the soul of an important person at their tomb. The church licenced middlemen, called pardoners, who took a commission from the church for their services as salesmen of pardons.

Longespée indulgence, Salisbury Cathedral Archives

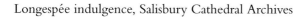

However, not all pardoners were genuine. Chaucer, in his *Canterbury Tales*, describes a pardoner who revelled in his own criminality and corruption by selling fake indulgences to gullible pilgrims for his own enrichment. The earliest of the Salisbury indulgences was one granted by Thomas Becket, Archbishop of Canterbury in 1169 to those who visited the relics at St. Peter's, Heytesbury, on the feast of Invention of the True Cross on 3 May. 1225 saw Stephen Langton, Archbishop of Canterbury, grant the first indulgence to help in the building of the new cathedral. In 1258, for the great ceremony of dedication of the cathedral, Pope Alexander IV and Archbishop Boniface both granted indulgences of 100 days. There are many indulgences for former canons and important secular citizens. A good example of this type was issued by Giffard, Bishop of Worcester, granting 40 days of indulgence to all those who offered prayers for the soul of William Longespée, 3rd Earl of Salisbury at his tomb in the Cathedral. Nine other bishops, on separate occasions, granted similar indulgences for William Longespée, an indication of his high status and the esteem in which he was held. In contrast the archives also have two indulgences for lowly hermits. The last indulgence in the archive issued was issued in 1536 by Pope Alexander VI granting 10,000 years' indulgence to penitents. The final document in the archive is a 1538 Injunction from Nicholas Shaxton, condemning pilgrimage and relics.

## Pilgrim Souvenirs in Salisbury

St James of Compostela with characteristic scallop shell, Salisbury Museum

The extensive collection of pilgrim badges in Salisbury Museum present the opportunity to study a wide variety of designs and materials. The badges were cast in moulds with lead or low quality pewter. Unfortunately no moulds for making St Osmund's badges have been found in Salisbury although it is probable that badges found in the city were made in the city. Having bought their badge, pilgrims would take it and carefully touch the shrine or reliquary with it. Sometimes the badge would be sprinkled with holy water from the shrine. It was believed these actions would impart the protective or healing power of the saint to the badge. The badge was then worn on the journey home for protection and as a public statement of a successful pilgrimage.[8] At the end of the journey there was a tradition for a badge to be deposited at a river crossing as a propitiatory or votive offering of thanks for a safe return home. The bulk of the large collection of badges in Salisbury came from the River Avon near Fisherton Bridge[9] and the leat feeding the Bishop's Mill. There was also a tradition to display a badge on or in the house of the pilgrim for its lasting protection of the household.[10] Other Pilgrim souvenirs included ampulla, whistles and rattles. An ampulla was a small lead or pewter bottle in which holy water from a shrine could be brought home. Pilgrims travelling in groups appear to have behaved rather like modern football supporters in making a lot of joyful noise[11] as they walked through towns approaching the holy site. This was augmented by the use of whistles and rattles. Examples of all of these have been found in Salisbury.

The tomb of Saint Osmund in Salisbury Cathedral

## Relics in Salisbury

The Catholic Church in medieval times taught that holy relics had special powers to connect the worshippers to the saints and to God. Relics offered protection and healing to the faithful. In Salisbury after the addition, in the early 14th century, of a towering spire, the whole church was protected by the insertion into the capstone of a small lead box containing a fragment of cloth, a relic of the Virgin.[12] In 1536 Master Thomas Robertson, the Cathedral Treasurer, listed many relics[13] among the treasures of the Cathedral: these included: 'A double cross Flory of Gold and silver: It stands upon four Lions, and has part of our Saviour's cross, with plates of gold and many stones of divers colours and pearls', the hair from the Apostle Saint Peter, an arm of St

Thomas Becket, a tooth of St Anne, the jaw bone of St Stephen, 'a piece of that St Andrew', a finger of St Agnes, a toe of St Mary Magdalene and even 'a pyx of ivory bound with copper conteyning the chain wherewyth St Catherine bound the Devil'. For centuries, pilgrims and local worshippers alike were awed by the splendour and range of pyxes, monstrances and saintly images containing relics on regular display or brought out for feast day processions.

## Pilgrim Destinations

The pilgrim badge collection in Salisbury Museum has examples associated with a wide range of destinations and over 30 saints. In this paper a limited number are selected as examples.

## St Osmund, Salisbury Cathedral

Bishop Osmund was buried in his cathedral at Old Sarum in 1099. Miracles were soon reported at his tomb and a local cult developed. His body was translated to Salisbury Cathedral in 1226. A number of efforts were made to achieve his canonisation following the failure of the first in 1228. Eventually, in 1457 after more miracles had been reported and a large donation given, Pope Callistus III approved.[14] A papal indulgence of three years was issued for pilgrims visiting Osmund's shrine on his feast day of 3rd December. The Pope insisted that Osmund's shrine should have 'a profusion of precious metals and jewels lavished on it' and so it was done. The tomb itself had six apertures allowing the pilgrims to reach inside and get closer to the saint. It should be noted that the presence of such a saint's relics in the cathedral would have been seen as a valuable source of income. Pilgrims would have been warmly

Pilgrim badge showing St Osmund supporting his cathedral with a pilgrim praying at his feet, Salisbury Museum

welcomed. Their offerings boosted the Chapter's income. Many badges related to Osmund's shrine in Salisbury Cathedral depict the head and shoulders of the saint wearing his mitre possibly copied from the 'great image of the holy St Osmund' created for his new shrine in 1457. Over 50 miracles were accredited to Osmund making him famous for his miraculous cures of madness, rupture, paralysis and toothache. There is also an unusual badge showing a pilgrim praying in front of Osmund having been miraculously transported by a vision of the Virgin, from Jaffa to Sarum in one day, to deliver a letter to Bishop Osmund.[15] It also shows him holding the cathedral and a document that could be the letter from Jaffa or a reference to his association with the Use of Sarum.

### Our Lady of Salisbury, Salisbury Cathedral.

Ordinary people living in Salisbury would look to Our Lady of Salisbury for help and protection. One of the costly images of Mary in the cathedral is described as 'Another grate and fair image of our Lady sitting in a chair, on her head is a crown, set about with stones and pearls'.[16] Not surprisingly in their moments of need they would call on her and on St Osmund. A number of local miracles were associated with them both. For instance in 1421 a Salisbury girl was accidentally impaled on a hot iron spit and thought to have died. Her family prayed to the Blessed Virgin and St Osmund and she was miraculously revived. The cathedral owned a range of relics associated with the Virgin including fragments of her clothes, her sepulchre, her hair and even her milk which would have drawn many local pilgrims to her shrine.[17] The fame of Our Lady of Salisbury spread to the Low Countries. Pilgrimages from Flanders to Salisbury were often imposed by courts as penalties for crimes[18]. Pilgrims were coming to Salisbury both as legal penitents as well as seeking the religious benefits of indulgences. A Salisbury Museum badge shows the Virgin as the crowned Queen of Heaven with the crowned infant Christ resting on her left hip as she holds a sceptre in her right hand.

Pilgrim badge showing the Virgin holding Christ as a child, Salisbury Museum

### Chapel of St Anne and The Blessed Virgin, East Gate of Salisbury Cathedral Close

In the mid 1300s a new chapel was built in the east gate of the Close. It was dedicated to St Anne and The Blessed Virgin. In 1354 a papal indulgence was granted for pilgrims visiting the chapel. A chapel devoted to the mother of the Virgin was seen as a preliminary station on the main pilgrimage to the shrine of Our Lady of Salisbury in the cathedral.[19]

### St Thomas of Canterbury Church, Salisbury

On the south wall of the nave overlooking the graveyard is a pilgrim's crucifix from the 14th century. Pilgrims from the south west counties paused here on their way to Canterbury. For Salisbury pilgrims this would have been the beginning of a journey to Canterbury. Inside the Church a powerful Doom painting dating from c1475 dominated the chancel arch. At its top a beautiful, sun drenched, celestial city was occupied by happy, repentant sinners. For those used to Salisbury's damp and misty climate and harsh social conditions it would have looked like the promise of paradise and a glimpse of heavenly perfection.

Lower down the picture, a terrifyingly devilish landscape of hell presented scenes of horrific suffering for unrepentant sinners struggling in everlasting fires. The public burning of Lollards (in the 1470s) in Salisbury Market Place[20] could only have heightened the citizen's fear of hell. This dramatic depiction contrasts the destination in the afterlife of Salisbury souls who repented their sins in this life and those who did not. This fearful message from the church may well have done much to encourage pilgrimage. Flanking the Doom painting are two large, bare footed, images of saints. On the right is Salisbury's own Saint Osmund, richly dressed and bearing a crozier. On the left is Saint James of Compostela wearing the traditional garb of a pilgrim with a scallop shell on his broad brimmed hat, a staff and a scrip. Does this image hint at the possibility of a Salisbury pilgrim paying for the creation of the Doom painting on a safe return from Spain? Perhaps.

Pilgrim badge of St Thomas of Canterbury, Salisbury Museum

## St Thomas's Shrine, Canterbury

Becket's disagreements with Henry II came to a head during the discussions over the Constitutions of Clarendon at the royal palace near Salisbury. After years in exile this ended in 1170 with Becket's murder in his own cathedral in Canterbury. The whole of Christendom was deeply shocked. Becket's shrine became the most visited pilgrimage site in England and one of the most important in Europe. Returning Salisbury pilgrims deposited their badges in the Avon in large numbers; 40 of them are in Salisbury Museum, indicating that Becket's shrine was the most visited by Salisbury pilgrims. Many of the badges are portraits of the saint wearing his mitre. Another shows him on a dappled horse. Yet another is a Canterbury bell embossed with his name and made from high grade pewter. Its clanging could have added to the general hubbub of public pilgrimage in Canterbury and Salisbury. Elsewhere in Wiltshire another Becket badge was incorporated into a 1470s church bell at Lyneham (a church associated with the nearby, Longespée funded, Bradenstoke Priory) to spread the power and influence of the saint each time it rang.

### St Edmund of Abingdon Church, Salisbury

Edmund Rich was Treasurer in Salisbury Cathedral before he became Archbishop of Canterbury. He was canonised in 1246. In the 1470s, during the Feasts of Michaelmas and the Annunciation, relics of St Edmund (his hand and ring) were displayed in the church. The Pope granted an indulgence for all those visiting the church at these times. Churchwardens' accounts talk of printing indulgences in English and paying a child to look after them at the feasts.[21] In 1480 this indulgence was suspended because of the Turks besieging the Knights of St John at Rhodes and the need to raise money directly for them.

### The Dominican Friary, Salisbury

The Dominicans or Black Friars started building their Friary in Fisherton in 1281 with help from the king. They remained active in the city for the next 250 years. This extensive site in Fisherton was home to 43 friars and had a church, a Prior's House, gardens and outbuildings. In 1393 Pope Boniface IX granted an indulgence 'Of 2 years and 2 quarantanes, to the faithful resorting to the house of the Black Friars of Fisherton, Salisbury out of devotion to St Peter, Martyr'. This indicates pilgrims were visiting here in the late 14th century and it is reasonable to believe that pilgrims had been coming to the Black Friars' House before this time. As well as their spiritual needs the pilgrims may have sought accommodation and perhaps medical help from the Friary's infirmary. Its church's aristocratic connections made it a desirable place in which to be buried. Sir Roger Beauchamp MP was buried here in 1406 alongside other high status Salisbury citizens. Sadly for us today, everything was destroyed at the Reformation. The modern Sainsbury supermarket has been built on the footprint of the medieval Friary, displaying a number of architectural references to its ecclesiastical predecessor (ie church-like towers, arches and cloisters).

### Trinity Hospital, Salisbury

In 1379 an indulgence was granted by the archbishop of Canterbury, and the bishops of London, Winchester, Durham, Ely, Lincoln, Salisbury, Exeter, Bath and Wells, Rochester, Hereford, and St. Asaph for those who gave charitable aid for support of the poor, weak, and destitute at the hospital founded by Agnes Bottenham.[22] The indulgence was used to attract offerings in the chapel of Trinity Hospital when pilgrims were in the city, visiting the cathedral, on the feast-days of the annunciation of the Blessed Virgin Mary and the nativity of St. John the Baptist, and of St. Michael the Archangel and the Holy Trinity.

## The Hospital of St John the Baptist and St Anthony

Recent research[23] suggests that this leper hospital was 500 metres east of Old Sarum on the Roman road to Winchester (today known as Ford Road). In 1388 John Waltham became the Bishop of Salisbury and in the same year granted an indulgence of 40 days to those making offerings at the leper hospital.

## St Edith's Shrine, Wilton Abbey

St Edith was the illegitimate daughter of the Saxon King Edgar and a Wilton nun, named Wulfryth. After her death in Wilton Abbey in 984 AD, she was canonised for her blameless life of good works. A cult developed at her shrine

and a precious relic, a fragment of a nail used on the True Cross, was donated to the Abbey. Legends abound of her miracles; King Canute[24] sailing back to Denmark was saved from a storm by St Edith and likewise Ealdred, Bishop of Worcester,[25] threatened by shipwreck in 1058 on a pilgrimage to the Holy Land was saved by a vision of St Edith. Wilton's royal connections ensured that the Abbey was one of the richest in the kingdom, enabling it to offer a high standard of care for pilgrims from England and Europe. In addition the Hospital of St Giles in Wilton added to the flow of pilgrims to the town in 1394 by offering 20 year indulgences to donors and visitors.[26] The Cathedral Archives have an indulgence granted for visiting Wilton Abbey on St Edith's

Pilgrim badge of St Edith of Wilton, Salisbury Museum

holiday, 14 September. Pilgrims from the south and east would pass through Salisbury on the way to Edith's shrine. Two St Edith badges have been found in Salisbury.

## St George's Chapel, Windsor

In 1473 Edward IV placed the Bishop of Salisbury, Richard Beauchamp, in charge of the rebuilding of St George's Chapel at Windsor. A famous relic of the True Cross attracted hundreds of pilgrims to the magnificent building. A roof boss shows the king and the Bishop of Salisbury praying in front of the relic. In an effort to increase pilgrim numbers still further Beauchamp obtained a Papal Bull allowing him to move the relics of a priest, John Schorn, from the village of North Marston to Windsor. Schorn was an exorcist with the power to trap the devil in a boot. His shrine proved to be very popular. Several Salisbury pilgrims returned with badges showing Schorn successfully restraining the devil. Salisbury Merchant Guild worked together in a confraternity that had St George as their patron saint. Salisbury pilgrims who visited Windsor to see relics of the saint returned with badges showing George killing the

Three pilgrim badges in Salisbury Museum.
From left to right: St George, John Schorn, King Henry VI

dragon. The St George's Chapel held several relics reputed to be from St George, including an arm, two fingers, a piece of his skull, and his heart. The latter was given by Emperor Sigismund on his creation as a Garter Knight in 1416. Some years after King Henry VI's violent death he was re-interred in St George's Chapel and although not canonised was venerated as a 'saintly king'. The Bishop of Salisbury created a tomb to facilitate pilgrimage. Pilgrims returning to Salisbury brought back a number of badges including a fine image of the king crowned and holding sceptre and orb. He is shown standing on a spotted antelope. A miracle associated with Henry occurred in 1484 when a man wrongly charged was hanged in Salisbury but saved by an image of the king supporting his feet.[27] The man was taken to the sanctuary of Blackfriars until a royal pardon arrived. In nearby Eton was the Church of Our Lady . Salisbury pilgrims visited and brought back badges.

## St Peter's, Rome
Rome has been the most important pilgrimage destination (after the Holy Land) since the early days of Christianity. But pilgrimage from Salisbury to Rome was especially arduous and time consuming. So perhaps it is not surprising that the Museum has only two examples of pilgrim badges from Rome depicting St Peter. One of them shows St Peter holding a key and a book. English pilgrims found accommodation in the English Hospice (later the English College) in Rome which kept records of their visitors. It is here that it is possible to see that amongst their guests are named a dozen or so pilgrims from Salisbury. These included the priests Walter Lonekyn and, Treasurer of Salisbury Cathedral, Richard Hilley (1503 -1533).[28]

## St James's Shrine, Compostela

The discovery of the relics of the Apostle St James the Greater, in Spain, created one of the most important pilgrim routes in Christendom. Salisbury Museum has a number of his characteristic scallop shell badges. Certainly the presence of these pilgrim badges in Salisbury tell us that Salisbury folk probably made the hazardous journey across the sea and returned safely. One badge in the Museum combines the image of the scallop shell with that of St James dressed in a voluminous cloak and wearing a big hat.

## Conclusions

Many historical accounts of Salisbury pay scant attention to pilgrimage in general and only occasionally mention St Osmund, saying his cult was never as famous or as popular as Thomas of Canterbury or James of Compostela and the numbers specifically visiting his shrine reflected this. Salisbury Cathedral on its website reports that 'there is no evidence that Salisbury ever became a major place of pilgrimage'. However, there is evidence of local veneration of Our Lady of Salisbury and the use by Salisbury citizens of saintly relics in their cathedral to help with their medical and social problems. An individual walking into the cathedral from the city, or surrounding villages was every much a true pilgrim as those arriving from all over Britain or distant Europe. In addition, Salisbury's geographical location ensured a steady trickle of additional pilgrims passing through the city on their way to other shrines. The flow of pilgrims was increased by Salisbury's own citizens intent on enhancing their entrance into heaven setting out as pilgrims to visit holy places, returning with badges to verify their journeys. The examination of the Cathedral's indulgences, relics and monuments, St Thomas's Church's Doom painting and the Museum's pilgrim badges illuminates the evident significance of pilgrimage in medieval Salisbury.

## Acknowledgements

The author wishes to thank the generosity of the following persons for their help: Emily Naish, Cathedral Archivist, for her assistance in examining indulgences and for photographing the Longespée indulgence. This image is being reproduced courtesy of the Dean and Chapter, Salisbury Cathedral. Adrian Green, Director of Salisbury Museum, for permission to use images of pilgrim badges. Nick Griffiths FSA, the artist who drew the images of the Salisbury pilgrim badges for his help and advice.

## Notes

1  Spencer, Brian.1990 *Salisbury Museum Medieval Catalogue part 2, Pilgrim Souvenirs and Secular Badges*, Salisbury & South Wiltshire Museum.

2  Dodsworth, William. 1814 *Cathedral Church of Salisbury*, Brodie & Dowding, 229

3  Matthew 25 31-46 A biblical account of the Day of Judgement.

4  Catechism of the Catholic Church 1999 (387, 1440 & 1471). See for a modern interpretation of the nature of sin and indulgences.

5  One of the earliest plenary indulgences was that granted by Pope Urban II in 1095 for those on the 1st Crusade.

6  Swanson, R N. 2007 *Indulgences in Late Medieval England, Passports to Paradise*. CUP

7  Wordsworth, Canon Christopher. 1913. Wiltshire Pardons or Indulgences *WAM* Vol XXXVIII, 15-33, records a list of 160 'indulgences and documents thereto relating, as granted to the Church of Salisbury . . . or registered by Bishops of Salisbury about the years 1170-1536' which provide examples of the people and issues involved with this process.

8  Spencer, 10

9  Spencer, 11

10  Spencer, 11

11  Spencer, 62

12  Gleeson White, 1898 *The Cathedral Church of Salisbury* Bell & Sons, 18

13  Wordsworth, C. 1901 *Ceremonies & Processions of the Church of Salisbury* CUP, 33-41, contains an extended named list of relics but without detailing the body part or object associated with the saint.

14  Malden, A R. 1901 *The Canonisation of St Osmund* Wilts Record Society

15  Ibid. 69

16  Dodsworth, 229

17  Wordsworth, 1901, 33

18  Spencer, 34

19  Webb, D. 2007 *Pilgrimage in Medieval England,* A & C Black, 106

20  Chandler, J. 2012 The Damned Bishop, *Sarum Chronicle* 12, 13

21  Swayne, H. 1896 *Churchwardens' Accounts of St Edmund's & St Thomas'* Wilts Record Society, xv

22  *VCH Wiltshire*, 3, 1956, 357-61.

23  Powell, Andrew, 2006 A possible site for the Hospital of St John the Baptist and St Anthony at Old Sarum, Salisbury, *WAM* 99, 213-20

24  Yorke, Barbara, 2004 Edith. *Oxford Dictionary of National Biography* OUP

25  Barlow, Frank (ed), 1992 *The Life of King Edward* OUP, 53

26  *VCH Wiltshire*, 3, 1956, 362-4.

27  Knox, Ronald, and Leslie, Shane, 1923 *The Miracles of Henry VI* CUP, 149-56

28  Hay, George, 2005 *The English Hospice in Rome* Gracewing, 99-190

# A Village Tale

## The Impact of War Office Ownership of Land on Salisbury Plain upon the Village of Imber between 1930 and 1950

## Stuart Wakefield

The village of Imber on Salisbury Plain was totally focussed upon agriculture and its population was in continual decline after 1851. At the end of the nineteenth century, the War Office commenced purchasing land on Salisbury Plain for military manoeuvres, while it was more than thirty years before land was acquired around Imber. Eventually, the villagers became War Office tenants, although the church, vicarage, chapel, school and public house remained in private hands. The War Office Salisbury Plain Committee had appointed its first Land Agent in 1902, and Imber residents wasted little time in presenting their new landlord with their problems.[1] Frank Wyatt was advised by the Land Agent on 5 March 1934 that it was not possible '. . . to erect cow-houses as the War Office will not approve any capital expenditure in the village . . .'.[2] Frank Carpenter sought to safeguard his tenancy and wrote on 13 June 1935 'I'm sorry I'm in arrears with rent. I seemed to have a string of bad luck last twelve months, . . . I will get it right as soon as possible, . . . I'm sending on one quarter of house rent'. In 1938, the War Department refurbished some village mud walled cottages and demolished others to make way for 16 new homes with running water, baths and outside bucket toilets.[3] On 14 May 1942, Sydney Dean wrote to local famers to propose a retirement gift for the Land Agent whose efforts after 30 years in post were judged as being untiring on behalf of the tenants, and '. . . it has always been possible to come to him with any difficulty, which he has always dealt with in the spirit of friendly cooperation'.[4]

During World War Two, Salisbury Plain was saturated with troops undergoing training, although Imber was largely ignored during the early years. However in 1943 the requirement to provide large areas for D Day training placed the War Office under considerable pressure, as numerous private properties needed to be requisitioned. The Americans required to maintain their fighting readiness, and the 3rd Armoured Brigade of 16,000 men was to arrive on Salisbury Plain in October 1943.[5] A War Office memorandum dated 24 September 1943 indicated that the North Hampshire Downs, the Pentridge Hills and the Imber area were being considered.[6] Time was of the essence, and within a week the Imber area was selected, primarily due to War Office ownership which would make it 'easier to evacuate tenants'.[7] Whilst this remark seems to trivialise the impending predicament of Imber villagers, it highlights a key tenet of the evacuation decision. In October, the Land Agent drew attention to issues that could result from Imber's evacuation by stressing the urgency of making an early decision at a time of dramatic food shortages, due to '. . . winter wheat being sown around Imber village and this labour, seed and money will be wasted if the scheme proceeds'.[8]

On 1 November 1943, all Imber tenants were called to a meeting in the school where each received a letter advising that that they should vacate their homes within six weeks as their tenancies were being terminated.[9] The letters were collected before the end of the day, which probably resulted from the stringent security that surrounded D Day preparations. The letter alluded

Sketch map of Salisbury Plain showing the position of Imber in relation to nearby towns, villages and river valleys

to '. . . increased training facilities . . . available for training by Dec 17th . . .', which could have compromised exceptionally sensitive issues, if publicised. The letter also included the phrase '. . . until the Imber area is again open for occupation . . .', which indicated that, at that time, the War Office had no plan to permanently exclude its tenants. Shortly after the eviction notices had been served, the Land Agent again took up the tenants' case in expressing concern that '. . . the last official sheep fair has been held, . . . rushed sales . . . would cause ill feeling amongst the farming community, which has so far been successfully avoided'.[10]

Notwithstanding censorship regulations, a newspaper reported that 3,000 people had to leave their homes in the south-west of England before year end, with apparent reference to various simultaneous evacuations associated with the D Day training requirement.[11] The newspaper suggested that villagers '. . . may be able to return to their homes and farms within a matter of months . . .' depending upon how the war went'. The report included an orchestrated stance, such as a claim by a County Council Chairman that a determined effort had been made to have another area selected, but higher authority ruled. The Minister for Agriculture expressed extreme regret regarding lost food production, but '. . . we have to win the war, and military priorities must take precedence'. An American General appealed to patriotism in stating that 'The hardship you are suffering will be compensated by the lives of Americans and Britishers that will be saved by what the men learn during their training in this area'. Another newspaper reported that the oldest Imber inhabitant, 88 year-old Mrs. Emily Goddard, stoically stated 'I were born here, and so were my six children, and they be granfers most on 'em now. I lived to die here, but must is with the King as must was with the Queen when I was young'.[12] The rector was most distressed as he struggled to pack his belongings and forlornly said that 'I haven't the faintest notion where to go, . . . if I were ten years younger I should try to get another parish'.-

On 28 November 1943, Imber St Giles's Church closed the day after the last wedding ceremony had been held, and, one week later, the last service was held in Imber Chapel.[13] Two Army Officers offered assistance with the removal and storage of personal possessions, and the villagers assumed that their absence would be relatively short as there was only minor concern for personal possessions mistakenly left behind.[14] Notwithstanding livelihoods having been ruined, personal circumstances impacted upon the ability of some to cope, such as having infants to consider and having husbands away in the military. Gladys Nash recalled that '. . . we had to do the best we could . . . we got a few pounds for vegetables in our garden . . . I know it sounds silly now to think that we left so willingly . . .'.[15] All 135 villagers had departed by the due date,

John Buckler's 1807 watercolour of St Giles's Church, Imber
(Illustration used with kind permission of the Wiltshire Museum, Devizes)

after 5200 sheep plus 70 head of cattle had been auctioned, and emotions were soothed by a general acceptance of the exigencies of wartime Britain. The villagers' way of life was carelessly scattered to satisfy the imperative of war, and residents departed to wherever and whatever refuge they could find. The final action was taken on 31 January 1944 by the issuing of an Order which closed 20,000 acres of the Imber Training Area to the public.[16]

In January 1944, the village blacksmith, Albert Nash, died and his remains were returned for burial at St Giles's Church. The Land Agent agreed to reimburse the costs associated with conveying the Sexton to dig and cover the grave, as well as for the hire of a hearse plus three cars from Devizes.[17] Mr Adlam was concerned that he had '. . . left a mangle and about 2 cwt of coal which we could not take'. Within a few days the Land Agent wrote to advise that he had taken '. . . the opportunity of checking on your garden. . . . the coal I estimate at 1 cwt, which is all dross and valueless. . . . the mangle I have had collected and is now at my Estate Yard at Durrington.' Mrs. Pearce wrote '. . . I left my 3 irons in the oven . . . would you please find any way in getting them for me, as I am in need of them'. In another letter, the Land Agent wrote to Mr Marsh to advise that 'The handbag to which you refer has been found and is held by me. When one of my Officers is near Kingston Deverell the opportunity will be taken to deliver it to you'.[18]

Five months after the evacuation, the War Office continued to communicate in a manner consistent with no policy being in place to preclude the reoccupation of Imber. It pessimistically observed that '. . . the chances of returning to Imber are getting more remote . . . buildings are already suffering a certain amount of damage from gunfire and weather'.[19] On 25 April 1945, in an attempt to quell concern over the evacuation, the War Office indifferently wrote of Imber villagers that '. . . these people are, I think, all satisfactorily absorbed in occupations or housed elsewhere'.[20] The War Office attitude began to harden, and, on VE Day, 8 May 1945, it adopted a position indicating the permanent use of the Imber Training Area in confirming that further similar actions in other locations were unnecessary.

A newspaper reported that the Bishop of Salisbury had received information of vandalism at Imber church '. . . committed during the occupation of the village by troops during the war'.[21] The allegation was contained in a letter written by Lord Long, who became prominent in the fight for the evacuated villagers to be permitted to return to Imber.[22] Lord Long also linked Imber to the ongoing and desperate food and housing crises by writing to the Secretary of State for War and the Ministers of Health and Agriculture to demand the immediate derequisition of Imber and the restoration of its 2,000 acres of derelict land to production; (this was a misinterpretation, as Imber, being War office property, had not been requisitioned). The newspaper subsequently reported Lord Long's claim that 'With the aid of one hundred Prisoners of War, Imber could house 200 people in ideal homelike conditions by November'.[23] It was later reported that Lord Long asked the Minister of Health if he thought it proper '. . . for this model village, on which £25,000 of the public's money was spent in 1938, to remain derelict'; (equal to £1,550,000 in 2017).[24]

On 11 September 1945, the War Office outlined its strategy in considering that, whilst the case for retaining Imber had been made, further action should be delayed.[25] It was unwilling to openly declare its intentions during the time of a national housing shortage which could leave it exposed to extensive criticism. It acknowledged that '. . . on balance of advantage, housing must at this time predominate, . . . if in say, two to three years, we could provide alternative accommodation, the problem would resolve itself'. Whilst the provision of alternative housing was not subsequently mentioned, it was concluded that some progress towards its objective could be made as '. . . we are to look ultimately to taking over the village as part of the training area . . . there is no reason why negotiations should not now be set on foot for the requisition of the five outstanding properties'.

To counter potentially negative publicity, the possibility of Imber being repopulated for a limited period was considered, although there was understandable unease over the time and effort that would be required to subsequently evict the residents a second time.[26] To emphasise such concerns, it was concluded that in such circumstances '. . . advantage will also doubtless be taken to improve the Church, Chapel, Vicarage, School, Pub etc., all with the object of making it impossible for us ever to use our own property . . .'.[27] On 23 October 1945, in the House of Commons, Mr Robert Grimston, (Conservative Member for Westbury), requested the Secretary of State for War to '. . . state the intentions of his Department with regard to the return of the civilian population to the village of Imber . . .'.[28] He was vaguely advised that 'The future of Imber village depends upon the type and intensity of the training allotted to the area in the post-war programme . . .', which reaffirmed that the War Office was unwilling to publicly acknowledge the decision that had been discussed a few weeks earlier. However, they were prepared to accept credit for having increased agricultural production, as, on 19 February 1946, the Secretary of State for War confirmed to Mr Grimston that the best use had been made of the area around the Imber Training Area for grazing and food production.[29]

Both local and national newspapers closely followed the Imber debate. In the House of Lords on 29 March 1946, Lord Long requested advice upon the compensation to be paid for damage suffered by Imber dwellings due to concussion; (this was a further misinterpretation, as Imber, being War Office property, was not a case for compensation).[30] He subsequently referred to the '. . . grave world shortage of foodstuffs . . .', when asking how many acres had been released and sown to corn. The Government confidently advised that '. . . only about 2,000 acres were now held for training in the Imber area, and precise instructions have been issued to troops regarding precautions to be taken to avoid damage to crops', and also acknowledged that '. . . the first priority was to feed the world'.[31] Farmers fallaciously referred back to conditions during the First World War when '. . . the area was an artillery range with shells dropping at the bottom of the garden, farming went on and villagers went about their lawful occasions without let or hindrance'.[32] In the House of Commons, Mr Christopher Hollis, (Conservative Member for Devizes), protested that land was being used for training not British, but Dutch troops, and that the Government had lost its reputation of being a worthy landlord.[33] In formally replying to Lord Long, the War Office defended the action taken in 1943, and reiterated its commitment that '. . . dispossessed tenants should have the first opportunity of returning, if and when the military have no further use for the village . . .' whilst confirming its stance that no assurance had ever been given that the Army would have no further use for the area.[34] In a newspaper interview, Lord Long was equally forceful in stating that it was '. . . in the nation's interest for Imber to be freed, . . . the houses are there, the land is there to grow food, . . .'.[35] Lord Long subsequently accused the Government of a breach of faith in promising to return land within the Imber Training Area to tenant farmers and then handing a portion of it over to establish a cement factory.[36]

Bertha Stokes wrote to agree with the conclusions drawn in an newspaper article written by Hugh Brandon-Cox, who had said of Imber that '. . . owing to the enormous expense involved to make it habitable, it would not be practical, . . . it is isolated and in a remote position for modern development as regards water supplies, sanitation, etc., which present day conditions demand'.[37] He also doubted that young people would choose to live in such a location that lacked recreation and amusement, and somewhat reluctantly concluded that Imber belonged in the past. Issues were highlighted that, if resolved, could reassure former residents, including the possibility of completely demolishing the village and rebuilding it on another site. In the same edition, Monica Hutchins also agreed with the article, and wrote that '. . . a great deal of nonsense has been written about Imber's remoteness and inaccessibility. It is just six miles from Warminster, a two cinema town with plenty of life'. She pointedly compared Imber's location with that of remote Exmoor villages which were at least ten miles from Porlock which had no organised entertainment.

On 8 April 1947, a War Office note indicated that its policy was hardening in doubting that Imber villagers would wish to return, and dismissively concluded that '. . . they have all got work elsewhere . . . the village is far from transport markets . . . restoration of the village as a community would be a matter of sentiment as opposed to a business proposition'.[38] The suggestion was also made, with reference to the ongoing housing crisis, that cottage fixtures, fittings and materials '. . . could be salved for use elsewhere . . . some of these materials have already been looted . . .'. One week later, the Army stated that 'the uninhabited Imber area . . . is vital for training purposes'.[39] A newspaper asked with reference to the proposed use of Imber for street fighting training, 'Why cannot mock villages be built for the purpose? Why must the housing shortage be sacrificed'?[40] The War Office was aware that debating such issues could expose its vulnerability, and did not respond.

On 31 August 1947, the War Office confirmed its aspiration to achieve an enlarged training area, and stated that 'When we put the area at the disposal

Seagram's Farm, one of the few remaining village buildings, now derelict. (Photo by Roy Bexon)

of the Americans for 'live' training, they pointed out how hampering these exceptions and restrictions were. This was incontestable and we accordingly cleared the village of inhabitants . . .'.[41] The Director of Military Training's objective was '. . . to undertake live training in a few large areas which would . . . make for greater efficiency and . . . greatly reduce the annoyance to the public from sporadic exercises all over the country'.[42] Imber was central to this strategy, as it was already War Office property, and to dispose of it would result in significant adjacent infrastructure being abandoned. On 17 November 1947, the War Office requested a ruling concerning the future of Imber to permit progress on the required By-Law for the associated road closure, as well as the allocation of existing houses for street fighting instruction plus the part-use of the Imber Training Area by the Ministry of Supply.[43]

On 10 October 1947, a conference was held at the Bishop's House, Salisbury, '. . . to consider the action to be taken to close Imber village in the event that the War Office decided that it was not to be re-inhabited'.[44] The specified purpose conflicted with the Department's policy, dated 11 September 1945, that there was no option for Imber villagers to return. It was agreed that the Home Office would be requested to '. . . grant an order closing the graveyard to any further burials'. This policy conflicted with the Land Agent's confirmation on 24 June 1944 of '. . . arrangements . . . by which the evicted inhabitants should be allowed to be buried in the churchyard'.[45] Other agreements concerned procedures for the de-consecration of the church and its maintenance, plus arrangements for relatives to visit the burial ground.[46] The War Office and the Salisbury Diocese subsequently agreed to the removal of the bells, font and old glass for safekeeping, and that the churchyard graves would not be disturbed.[47]

By 12 January 1948, the War Office sensed that it was winning the Imber debate and robustly defended its stance. The Director of Military Training confidently asserted that 'The case for the retention of Imber village by the Army for training purposes seems to me to be quite unanswerable. It is quite useless to anyone else and is of great use to us'.[48] On 6 April 1948, the policy was unquestionably in the public domain when Mr Daniel Lipson, (Independent Member for Cheltenham), asked the Secretary of State for War if he would reconsider his Department's decision not to release the village of Imber for civilian use.[49] In reply, it was stated that there were no new factors to take into account that would support the case for a review of the decision. Colonel Alan Gandar-Dower, (Conservative Member for Penrith and Cockermouth), then asked '. . . if the War Office was satisfied that Imber was a suitable area for street fighting, as it was not substantially built up', and was advised that 'In choosing an area for training of this kind we cannot select what, for purely military reasons, would be perhaps the ideal area'. General Sir George Jeffreys, (Conservative Member for Petersfield), asked what was the advantage for the Army in retaining Imber, and was advised that '. . . the number of places where there are the necessary facilities and where people are not in occupation must be extremely limited . . . it would not be a reasonable proposition, on merely economic grounds, to make it habitable again'.

A newspaper lamented 'It is Wiltshire's misfortune that, possessing as it does the vast area of Salisbury Plain, the War Office should have refused consistently to release the Imber area which lies in the middle of an otherwise uninhabited stretch of land'.[50] Another report quoted the last resident of Imber Court, Robert Whistler, who confirmed that he had attended the meeting on 1 November 1943, and did not believe that the War Office had pledged that villagers would be permitted to return.[51] He acknowledged that the point was raised, and the representative had advised that, in all probability, villagers should be back in Imber within three to six months, but he did not take that as a pledge. He also confirmed that representatives had visited some of the older residents and commiserated with them, although he considered that they would have resisted eviction if they had been advised that they would never return. The same report also quoted former Imber resident, Mr Frank Carpenter, who had also attended the meeting and stated that '. . . we were told by the Army Officer we were to return to Imber', and his recollection was corroborated by both Mrs. Wyatt and Mrs. Meaden.

A newspaper reported on 11 April 1948 that Lord Long had reason to believe that '. . . Imber will be the target for an atom bomb, . . . released by aircraft twenty miles away in the hope that it will drop on empty Imber', to which the Ministry of Supply advised that this report was without foundation.[52] This statement should be viewed in the light of general unawareness, at the time, of the destructive capability of atomic weapons. A subsequent newspaper report of proceedings in the House of Lords advised that Lord Long had asked the Minister of Civil Aviation '. . . for an assurance that, before any bombing occurred in this area, relatives would have an opportunity for their loved ones, buried in the churchyard, to be removed at public expense'.[53] The Minister of Defence subsequently stated in the House of Commons that the Ministry of Supply needed parts of the training area as ranges for various tests and trials, and that no live bombs would be dropped.[54] Mr Grimston noted that '. . . this is the first time this information has been made public, . . . if high-level bombing is indulged in, a short error of calculation may cause damage to life and property outside of the area'. On 16 April 1961, the Minister of Supply confirmed that experimental bomb dropping had been carried out on the Imber training area on 134 days during the previous 12 months.[55]

The War Office engendered criticism over its Imber policy from the Ministry of Town and Country Planning in a formal communication, dated 7 May 1948, which stated that before the war '. . . the use was such that people could live in Imber village, whereas the use now proposed is such that people cannot live in the village, . . . the whole attitude of the War Department to the matter is wrong'.[56] There was concern that the War Office had failed to present the change of use of the Imber Training Area for discussion at the Inter Departmental Committee. The Ministry also referred to the view of the Council for the Preservation of Rural England, as expressed in the Minutes of its meeting on 13 April 1948.[57] It was recorded that, whilst little would be gained from pressing for a Public Inquiry, '. . . the procedure followed by the War Office seemed open to serious criticism . . .'.[58] The Council's position was underscored at the subsequent Annual Meeting of the Wiltshire Branch where the President stated that 'The question of Imber had been settled . . . it was no good having regrets but he would like to say that of all those he had seen and spoken to, not many would like to go back to Imber'.[59]

The War Office maintained a tight control over civilian access to Imber, and villagers felt indignant at having to formally request to return to the village.[60] However, from 1955, villagers were permitted to return in groups, and St Giles's Church was opened for services which allowed graves of loved ones to be tidied. On 31 December 1960, the 1939 Defence of the Realm Act expired, and the Army's authority to close roads in the Imber Training Area

St Giles's Church, restored and used for occasional services, protected by barbed wire.
(Photo by Roy Bexon)

on the grounds of safety was challenged by Councillor Austin Underwood of
Amesbury Rural Council. A Public Inquiry was demanded into a provisional
Ministry of Transport Draft Order to permanently prohibit access to the roads.
In 1961, the Association for the Restoration of Imber was formed and protests
were held at Imber. A High Court legal challenge failed, and all remaining
hopes were pinned on the Public Inquiry at Trowbridge on 3 October 1961.
The only issue considered was whether or not the Rights of Way should be
closed, and the final decision was to be made by the Minister of Transport. In
January 1962, the Ministry stated that the Draft Order for the closure of Imber
Training Area roads was to stand, and, in a conciliatory gesture, the War Office
agreed to provide public access to the Training Area roads for up to fifty days
each year.

# Bibliography

**Archival Sources**
**History Centre, Amesbury**
unreferenced file Imber
**Museum of English Rural Life, Reading**
SR CPRE A/7   Minute Book of the Council for the Preservation of Rural England, Executive Committee 1947 to 1950
**The National Archives, Kew**
WO 32/16679   War Department Estate, Imber, Wiltshire, use as battle training area, 1943 to 1948
WO 32/17163   Imber Training Area, Salisbury Plain, acquisition of village and proposed maintenance programme, 1947 to 1973
WO 33/236   Minutes of the proceedings of the Salisbury Plain Committee, 1897 to 1902
**Wiltshire and Swindon Archives, Chippenham**
1284/71   Correspondence and press cuttings relating to Imber, 1948 to 1969
2860/3   2860 - Austin Underwood Papers, The Association for the Restoration of Imber, Official letters, Committee minutes, byelaws and other papers relating to closure of Imber. 1944 to 1989
L7/310/1 Purchase of cottages and blacksmith's shop on the Imber estate, 1930 to 1943
L7/310/2 Claims for removal expenses from properties in Imber, 1941 to 1944
**Wiltshire Museum, Devizes**
MSS.3803 4 albums containing a history of Imber, Wiltshire prior to its evacuation in 1943; includes photographs, newspaper cuttings and a typed commentary, regarding local families, businesses, buildings and wildlife, by E.D. Hooper of Devizes, Wiltshire

**Newspapers**
*News Chronicle*
*Sunday Express*
*Sunday Pictorial*
*The Times*
*Wiltshire Gazette*

**Books**
Corden C., *The Plain, Life on Salisbury Plain from the 1890s to the present day*, Halsgrove
Daniels P. and Rex Sawyer, *The Archive Photographs Series: Salisbury Plain,* Tempus Publishing
Harrison G.A., *Cross Channel Attack*, (U.S Army Center of Military History: Library of Congress Catalog Card Number: 51-61669, 1951, http://www.history.army.mil/html/ books/007/7-4-1/index.html
Sawyer R., *Little Imber on the Down,* Hobnob Press

**Websites**
*East Anglian Daily Times*, Villages remember wartime evacuation; http://www.eadt. co.uk/news/villages_remember_wartime_evacuation_1_188940
National Archives: 'Public inquiry guidance'; http://www.nationalarchives.gov.uk/ information-management/manage-information/public-inquiry-guidance
UK Parliamentary Papers; http://parlipapers.proquest.com.libezproxy.open.ac.

WW2 People's War, Breckland Exodus-The Forced Evacuation of the Norfolk Battle Area 1942; http://www.bbc.co.uk/history/ww2peopleswar/stories/62/a3258362.shtml

## Notes

1   National Archives, file WO 33/236.
2   WSA, file L7/310/1.
3   Daniels and Sawyer, *The Archive Photographs Series* p. 36.
4   Wiltshire Museum Archives, file MSS.3803.
5   2.88 million troops were assigned to the invasion; Gordon A. Harrison, *Cross Channel Attack,* U.S Army Center of Military History: Library of Congress Catalog Card Number: 51-61669, 1951, p. 158, footnote 1, <http://www.history.army.mil/html/books/007/7-4-1/index.html>, accessed August 2016.
6   National Archives, file WO 32/16679.
7   The War Office already had experience of evacuating owners from requisitioned land in locations including Sudbourne and Iken - <http://www.eadt.co.uk/news/villages_remember_wartime_evacuation_1_188940>, and Thetford - <http://www.bbc.co.uk/history/ww2peopleswar/stories/62/a3258362.shtml>, accessed September 2016.
8   National Archives, file WO 32/16679.
9   Sawyer, *Little Imber on the Down,* p. 97.
10  National Archives, file WO 32/16679.
11  *Wiltshire Gazette*, 18 November 1943.
12  *News Chronicle*, 11 November 1943.
13  Sawyer, p. 103.
14  Chris Corden, *The Plain,* (Tiverton: Halsgrove, 1998), p. 83.
15  Sawyer, p. 101.
16  WSA, file 2860/3.
17  WSA, L7/310/1.
18  WSA, file L7/310/2.
19  National Archives, file WO 32/16679.
20  National Archives, file WO 32/16679.
21  *The Times*, 29 August 1945.
22  3rd Viscount Long of Wraxall retained the Westbury seat for the Conservatives from 1927 to 1931.
23  *The Times*, 4 September, 1945.
24  *The Times*, 13 September 1945.
25  National Archives, file WO 32/16679.
26  National Archives, file WO 32/16679.
27  Ushers Brewery maintained the Bell Inn licence for many years before selling the property to the War Office for £3500 on 8 May 1959; Amesbury History Centre, file Imber.
28  Robert Grimston MP retained the Westbury seat for the Conservatives from 1931 to 1964; <http://parlipapers.proquest.com.libezproxy.open.ac.uk/parlipapers/result/pqp documentview?accountid=14697&groupid=95579&pgId=1c58d9c5-d639-4169-b752-de2d06d33141&rsId=157C82B87DC>, accessed September 2016.
29  <http://parlipapers.proquest.com.libezproxy.open.ac.uk/parlipapers/docview/t71.d76.cas5cv0419p00007?accountid=14697>, accessed September 2016.
30  *The Times*, 27 March 1946.

31  *The Times*, 10 May 1946.

32  *Wiltshire Gazette*, 23 May 1946.

33  NATO was formed in 1949, and this comment predated European defence cooperation; *Wiltshire Gazette*, 11 July 1946.

34  *Wiltshire Gazette*, 15 August 1946.

35  *Wiltshire Gazette*, 30 August 1946.

36  The factory would supply key building materials; *The Times*, 27 November 1946.

37  *Wiltshire Gazette*, 29 April 1948.

38  National Archives, file WO 32/17163.

39  WSA, file 1284/71.

40  *Sunday Pictorial*, 4 April 1948.

41  National Archives, file WO32/16679.

42  After World War Two, some considered that no troop training should take place in Britain and it should only be carried out in the colonies.

43  The Ministry of Supply was established in 1939 to coordinate the design, inspection, research and experimental work related to the supply of munitions, clothing and other stores to the War Office and Air Ministry; National Archives, file WO32/16679.

44  National Archives, file WO32/16679.

45  WSA, file L7/310/1.

46  St Giles's Church remains consecrated and the burial ground remains available to former Imber residents.

47  *Wiltshire Gazette*, 7 April 1949.

48  National Archives, file WO 32/17163.

49  <http://parlipapers.proquest.com.libezproxy.open.ac.uk/parlipapers/result/pqpdocumentview?accountid =14697&groupid=95579&pgId=731e4c3a-cb61-4b4d-879a-930f5254573&rsId=157C8A7B935#t0020>, accessed September 2016.

50  *Wiltshire Gazette*, 1 April 1948.

51  *Wiltshire Gazette*, 8 April 1948.

52  *Sunday Express*, 11 April 1948.

53  *Wiltshire Gazette*, 15 April 1948.

54  *The Times*, 6 May 1948.

55  <http://parlipapers.proquest.com.libezproxy.open.ac.uk/parlipapers/result/pqpdocumentview? accountid=14697&groupid=95579&pgId=aae344f6-b692-4055-b630 0bee9914eb72&rsId=15922201BE1#t0009>, accessed September 2016.

56  National Archives, file WO32/17163.

57  Museum of English Rural Life Archives, file SR CPRE A/7.

58  Public inquiries investigate issues of serious public concern; <http://www.nationalarchives.gov.uk/information-management/manage-information/public-inquiry-guidance/>, accessed October 2016.

59  *Wiltshire Gazette*, 20 May 1948.

60  A comprehensive account of related events after 1950 can be found in Rex Sawyer's *Little Imber on the Down*, pp. 119 to 157.

Sincere thanks for contributions and guidance in developing this paper are due to Dr J Kirkaldy plus many Curators and Archivists who freely gave me their time and provided access to their valued documents.

# Barney Norris – novelist, playwright and poet

## interviewed by John Cox

The present is only ever one day long
*(Five Rivers Met on a Wooded Plain)*

Barney Norris was born in Sussex in 1987 and after moving to Salisbury attended Bishop Wordsworth's School and was a leading member of Stage '65, the Playhouse Youth Theatre. After his BA (Hons) from Keble College, Oxford and MA (Hons) from Royal Holloway, University of London, he founded the theatre company "Up in Arms", of which he is the co-artistic director.

For his debut full-length play *Visitors* he won the Critics Circle Award and the Offwestend Award for Most Promising Playwright and was also shortlisted for the Evening Standard Theatre Awards for Most Promising Playwright and the Writers' Guild of Great Britain award for Best Play. *Visitors* was named as one of the plays of 2014 by the *Guardian* and the *Evening Standard*. His next play, *Eventide*, was named as one of the plays of 2015 by The *Times*, The *Stage* and the *Arts Desk*, in the same year that he was named as one of the 1,000 Most Influential Londoners by the *Evening Standard*.

His first non-fiction book *To Bodies Gone: The Theatre of Peter Gill* was published by Seren in 2014, and his first pamphlet of poetry, *Falling*, was published by Playdead Press in 2013. Barney's debut novel, *Five Rivers Met on a Wooded Plain,* was published by Transworld (Doubleday) in 2016 to widespread critical acclaim. It was a Waterstones and Foyles Book of the Month and *Guardian, Daily Mail* and *Evening Standard* Book of the Year, and saw him named as the Literature nominee for the South Bank Sky Arts Sunday Times

'Wonderful . . . I was hooked from the first page. It's the real stuff' Michael Frayn

FIVE RIVERS MET ON A WOODED PLAIN

Barney Norris

'One of our most exciting young writers' *The Times*

Breakthrough Award. His second novel *Turning for Home* is to be published in January 2018.

At the time of this interview (March/ April 2017), performances were under way of Barney's new play, *Echo's End* on the main stage of Salisbury Playhouse, which commissioned it, and rehearsals for another play by him *While We're Here* which was scheduled for the Salberg Studio in June.

★★★

JC    In her review of your novel *Five Rivers Met on a Wooded Plain*[1] Suzy Feay wrote: 'All of the characters are acutely conscious of the passage of time and missed chances.' While most narrative writing deals with the determining factors of the past, would you say that your writing seems especially concerned with your characters' past lives?

BN    Of course I can only speak for my own work's preoccupations, and how those appear in the context of other people's work is difficult for me to be clear about, but I certainly think you're right on this. I'm fascinated by ideas of cultural inheritance – it becomes clearer and clearer to me that inheritance is a theme I always visit. What gets passed down, and what gets lost.

In the plays *Visitors, Eventide, Echo's End, While We're Here*, and in the novels *Five Rivers* and *Turning For Home* a character has to sell their home, or give up the lease, or otherwise shape their identity around the home of which they have come into possession. The property inheritance preoccupation is interesting because it's more easily analysed, of course, than the question of how our past lives shape our present. That's such a big question as to be incalculable. I think selling or buying houses always goes in the story as a marker that I'm trying to talk about what gets passed down. Or not, as the case may be.

JC You commented in an interview [2] about how in your first full length play *Visitors* you tried 'to create a portrait of an England I felt was presently receding, because I think the writer's job is always to document cultures before they disappear...' Do you think you succeeded?

BN    That would probably be a bold claim! I think any piece of work that makes it to the public, and is received with a sense of recognition (as I like to think that play was), can be said to have saved something from the fire. Because it will all go, everything around us, it will all have disappeared one day, so there's nothing you can name that doesn't need recording. If it struck someone as true at the time people first saw it, then it's likely to have done a job on that front. I know with absolute certainty that I could never succeed absolutely at the task. I'm always struck by this walking through Salisbury. To tell the full story of Salisbury, you would need to record everything that ever happened in every room. And I never will, of course, that's impossible. When I walk down Exeter Street and think of all the things that happened behind those different doors that will all one day be forgotten, it breaks my heart really. They were once like our lives now, and then it will be as if they never happened. But there's a beauty to failing at that too, I think.

JC I think you've exactly caught this feeling in *Echo's End* when Anna says: 'No one will know about us, will they? A hundred years will pass and we will have lived and died, and there'll be no sign of us. Only the trees will remember.'

In *Five Rivers Met on a Wooded Plain* the geography of Salisbury and its five rivers is in evidence. How far are the lives of the five characters affected by it?

BN    All our lives are shaped by the conditions we're born into. That's probably the most important observation fiction makes, one of its great functions as a medium is to explore that truth. The great prose poem expressing that truth is *Jude the Obscure*. Hardy was able to illustrate that deafeningly important lesson more clearly than, say, I am, because he lived when social mobility was difficult. So he can really hammer it home. But the fact that novelists in the twentieth and early twenty-first centuries wrote when social mobility increased doesn't mean they stopped writing books that proved the conditions of our birth shape the whole of our lives – it was just that one of the conditions of their births was social mobility.

JC That shift certainly comes home to the character of Arthur, the smallholder, in *Visitors* as he talks to a new carer and he compares his life with his wife Edie to that of his son Steve:

'It's been such a change in our lifetime, how people fix up their lives. For me and Edie, I don't think it entered our heads we'd do anything different to this. It's what we were born to, isn't it. Then for Steve when he left, my son decided he didn't want to farm you see..... That was a big fight we had then. But in the end we thought, that's probably what progress looks like, because he can have a better life now. And perhaps he has.'

BN    There's nothing in *Five Rivers* that isn't a result of the interaction between a human life and a landscape. Right down to the fact that the book happens at all – as with all first person narratives, a question lurks behind the pages as to whom the book is speaking. The answer is that I used to walk half an

Barney Norris. (photo by Jay Brooks)

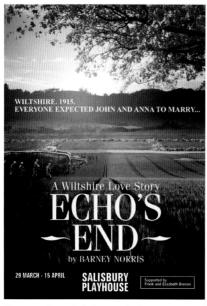

Poster for *Echo's End* (courtesy of Salisbury Playhouse)

hour into school every day, and half an hour home, and I used to fill that time with talking to myself (not always out loud, though probably more often than was entirely respectable!). Wiltshire is a land of long commutes – isolated parishes that haven't bled into one another because of the Plain. People sit on buses or walk or drive for lengths of time in Wiltshire – they commute from Salisbury to Swindon; they live in Amesbury and go to Burgate; they walk from Harnham to St Mark's roundabout, because for all that there's a bus network, it's not quicker than Shanks' pony, really, you always have to change in the Market Square, don't you? So the entire scaffolding of that book lies hidden in the landscape – in the long stretches of time that people spend alone in Wiltshire, alone with their thoughts, alone with the two selves that make up all of us, the real and the dream, which are always in conversation of course, but whose conversation becomes more audible when you're walking an hour a day to and from school with a trombone on your back and a bag of school books over your shoulder.

JC *Echo's End* is set on the edge of Salisbury Plain in 1915 and tells the story of two families and the radical changes which altered their lives and the identity of their county forever. Critical reviews of this first production have been predominantly favourable, a number appreciating your engagement with the past: '… it is infused with an august Rupert Brooke wistfulness, a mixture of melancholic nostalgia and hazy remembrance.' …. 'he shows the long reach of history' …. 'it looks through the long lens of history' [3]

With *Echo's End* how far have you actively included local history in your writing as well as your own experience?

BN   I'm in the camp of Robert Frost and Edward Thomas on this one – I make almost nothing up. And as you point out, that leads to a blend of autobiography and, I suppose, folk song collection, as the way you make a story. I refer to it as 'dredging the hedgerows'. *Echo's End* has been a step change for me in privileging local history equally alongside personal experience – before then, I had so much to pass on that I first heard from my family that tended

The cast of *Echo's End* at Salisbury Playhouse (photo by Helen Murray)
Left to right: Robin Soans (Jasper); Oliver Hembrough (Jack); Sadie Shimmin (Margaret); David Beames (Arnold); Katie Moore (Anna); Tom Byrne (John)

to take up the lion's' share of the work. But while there are still stories from my family in that play, I've also searched more widely, through Hardy, A. G. Street, Richard Jefferies, Edward and Helen Thomas, W. H. Hudson, all great chroniclers of Wiltshire, and Baring-Gould, and Sharp, and Clare, people who could show me the temper of the times. I'm reading George Deacon's *John Clare and the folk tradition* at the moment, and he draws a crucial distinction in that book, pointing out that folk traditions are never 'passed on', that's far too passive a form of words – they are 'handed down'. Knowledge has to be actively imparted to the following generations, or it is lost. I explored Salisbury's museums and I am also indebted to insights from contemporary military historians Neil Hall and T. S. Crawford, and to Richard Osgood the Senior Historic Advisor with the Defence Infrastructure Organisation.

As I wrote *Echo's End* I thought more and more about taking responsibility for the cultural heritage I had been asked to set a play amongst – collecting as much life as I could in one place, and giving it to the people it belongs to, who may or perhaps may not be aware of the things that happened before they were born, that have undoubtedly led to them, have formed them. So local history has become a very active preoccupation over the course of that commission, and now I'm in love with the project of collecting the lives that came before us, and giving them back to the people they led to. I have a plan for a sequel to *Echo's End*, which I have to get someone to do, because there's just so much to say, far more than I'll ever say, but now I've got stuck in I want to keep on with the attempt. It's an immense gift Gareth Machin, the artistic director at Salisbury, has given me, this new access to a whole new function of drama and storytelling, and a whole new palette to work with. At first I cursed him, because it was a nightmare, I've had to read millions of words to write even a two hour play because to do anything less is an act of such cultural vandalism, but it's like everything else – do your ten thousand hours and you start to reap rewards.

JC Have you thought about Stonehenge – or Avebury or Woodhenge – as settings or features of your writing?

BN    That's such an interesting question. I've skirted round them to date for two reasons – firstly, because of *Tess of the d'Urbevilles*. I haven't gone near the clergy in Salisbury because Golding wrote *The Spire*, and I feel similarly about Stonehenge. The greatest novelists in the culture, bar none, set their greatest books on our doorstep, and if you're going to put yourself out there and ask to be compared with those novels, you've got to be really sure you have something to say! Secondly, I avoided the greatest hits of the county because I feel like they've somewhat limited the experience of the ordinary person, in the popular imagination. *Tess* and *The Spire* and Jez Butterworth's play *Jerusalem* are in love with the potential of Wiltshire as metaphor, but for people who live here, Wiltshire isn't a metaphor, it's a place in which they get through all the challenges in the course of a life. I wanted to look at the less glamorous channels we all run through as well.

But the more I think about taking responsibility, about storytelling as saving things from the fire and articulating inheritance, the more I wonder whether Stonehenge needs to turn up some time, in a more meaningful way than in the opening of *Five Rivers*. When you start writing, you wouldn't dare in a million years assume the role of 'keeper of the collective memory', or anything like that. You're a kid trying to avoid getting a real job, that's the start for a writer. But there does come a point, if you manage not to need a real job, when you realise you have this enormous privilege, which is having acres of time to read. And as a result of that, you know more odd facts than many people, because you spend hours and hours immersed in trivia. And that does lead you to thinking about how you might deserve and earn that privilege, if that makes sense – and the idea of trying to gather and articulate things that people might not otherwise come across does undoubtedly spring up.

## Notes

1    *The Financial Times* 8 July 2016
2    *The Independent* 30 November 2014
3    *The Stage/ The Guardian/ What's On Stage* All 3 April 2017

# One hundred years ago: Salisbury Cathedral in a time of war

*Extracts from the minutes of the Salisbury Dean & Chapter meetings in 1917*

## John Elliott

The minutes of the of the Dean & Chapter meetings reveal the details of their responsibility for running a large ecclesiastical organization and property portfolio. As we saw in the last issue of *Sarum Chronicle* 1916 was a time of financial worries such that the Dean & Chapter suggested to the Ecclesiastical Commissioners that there was 'reason to think that the Salisbury Chapter is the poorest in England (with the possible exception of Chichester).'[1]

These financial worries continued in 1917 and the income from cathedral owned properties in the Close became absolutely critical to the continued operation of the cathedral. As a result the discussions of the Dean & Chapter were dominated by such property matters despite the very significant international events that were taking place elsewhere.

1917 was the year when the battle of Vimy Ridge was fought, the hundred day battle of Flanders began and the British eventually won at Passchendaele. It was also the year when the Russian Revolution started and when Britain acknowledged the need for a home for the Jewish people in Palestine.

The conflict was having an effect in Salisbury as several members of staff left the cathedral to join the war effort. At the 2 January meeting a £5 War Bonus was agreed for four of the lay vicars (Messrs Tyack, Noyes, Dyson and Case) and this was repeated at the 4 December meeting when £10 each was awarded to Messrs Tyack, Noyes and Dyson and a War Bonus of £7 10 0d was agreed should be paid to Mr Freemantle the senior verger. The inclusion of Mr Case in the January award but his omission from that made in December suggests that he may have perished in the fighting. For the cathedral the departure of almost half of the lay vicars must have had a dramatic impact on the cathedral's ability to deliver challenging choral arrangements.

There was also a considerable concern about aircraft, and the damage they could inflict. Flying took place from Old Sarum and several airfields on Salisbury Plain. Presumably the cathedral authorities were worried about German Zeppelin raids and later Gotha bombers being attracted to the area.

On 6 February the Chapter Clerk provided statements of the chancels that the Dean & Chapter were responsible for repairing, the amount of any insurance against fire, and a separate statement listing the insurances held against damage by aircraft.

A few days later, on 13 February, the Dean & Chapter noted that the Government would be rebating 50% of aircraft insurance premiums after 1 March, and decided to lapse the policy with the Ecclesiastical Insurance Office for £58,000 from 14 February. They asked that the Clerk confirm coverage from 14 February to 1 March with Lloyds, providing the premium did not exceed £5.

However, despite these changes insurance premiums of £237 1s 5d were paid for cover against fire and aircraft damage to the cathedral and any of the properties in the Close, though £153 14s 11d of this was recovered from the occupants of the houses.

During the year the cathedral ran with a deficit of £169 16s 2d. Income was £2,217 17s 2d with expenditure of £2,387 13s 4d. (This is equivalent to a deficit of about £13,500 in current money).

The income was dominated by rents from the 22 houses and 5 cottages within the Close and De Vaux Place. The rent for a house was about £100, and £12 for a cottage. These rents produced income of £1,571 2s 4d. The rents from some small parcels of land added another £56 1s 8d giving a total income from property of £1,627 4s 0d. This accounted for 73% of total income. Hence the great focus on property matters that dominated most meetings of the Dean & Chapter, and no doubt also consuming much of the Dean's thinking time. Collections and donations amounted to only £154 16s 2d.

The Dean between 1907 and 1919 was William Page Roberts who was born in Liverpool in 1836. His father was a confectioner and dining room keeper. He was one of three children, was educated at Cambridge, ordained in 1862

William Page Roberts, Dean of Salisbury. (c) Salisbury Museum collection 5264

and commenced his priesthood in Merseyside before becoming vicar of St Peter's, Vere Street, Marylebone, London.[2] He was appointed as a Canon of Canterbury cathedral in 1895, and retained that position until he was appointed to Salisbury in 1907. After leaving Salisbury he retired to Shanklin on the Isle of Wight and died there in 1928. This was a not untypical career for a member of the clergy, but one that provided little preparation for the role of Salisbury Dean and its heavy dominance upon business matters.

A full analysis of the cathedral's receipts and payments is given in Appendix 1 and a list of the properties, occupiers and annual rent payment in 1917 in Appendix 2.

During the year the lease of No 16 proved slightly problematic. On 2 January the Chapter noted that the lease on Canon Dimont's house – No 16 – had been surrendered. Canon Charles Tunnacliff Dimont (1872-1953) was vice principal of Wells Theological College from 1909 to 1913 when he became principal of Salisbury Theological College, a post he held until 1937. He later became chaplain to St Nicholas Hospital. The 1911 census shows him living near Wells with his wife, two daughters and 3 servants. Debrett's says that eventually he had four children and lived at 23 The Close. His wife, Nora Frances Haydn Green, was a sister of Sir Francis Haydn Green and their father had been a Lieutenant of the City of London.

On 6 February 1917 the Dean & Chapter approved an application from a Mrs John Carpenter who wished to assume the tenancy of No 16 at the same rent. The minutes of 5 April confirmed that this had happened, though something clearly went wrong as on 10 May it was agreed that a Miss Kingsbury who lived at No 7 should take on the house and be allowed £25 towards the cost of decoration and internal repairs. It was also agreed that Canon Dimont be allowed half the cost of some new gates that he had erected as long as this did not exceed £3 10 0d. The problems did not cease there as on 5 June it was agreed that the rent would be increased by £5 per year to cover the cost of redecoration.

On 3 August Miss Kingsbury surrendered the lease on No 7 and it was agreed to let the house to Mr A A G. Malet for three years, though on 5 November the Dean & Chapter agreed to remit two weeks rent because of delays in completing internal repairs.

Helen Mary Kingsbury (1858-1929) was an unmarried lady of independent means who was born at Savernake. The 1911 census shows her at 7 The Close with a companion (Lucy Brine), a visitor and 5 servants. She had been disabled in a carriage accident but hosted Sunday gatherings. There were special treats for the choristers and in summer she rented a cottage in Savernake Forest where the boys went on Wednesdays.[3]

There was also a problem with the drains for No 8. On 10 May Mr Paget, secretary of the training college, wrote informing the Dean & Chapter of problems and Mr Messenger, the Clerk of Works, was directed to carry out an inspection. On 5 June he reported that he had inspected the drains and found no fault. However, on 3 August the Chapter agreed to undertake repairs to the drains which pass under the house, on condition that the Rev J W C Wand, who occupied the adjoining house, contribute half the cost. It was also agreed that the rent paid by the training college be increased by £5 for two years so as to defray the Dean & Chapter's costs.

Helen Kingsbury (right) and Lucy Brine (left).

In April Mrs Murray who lived in Marefield in De Vaux Place was told that she could end her lease with the usual 6 months notice as long as she had found a replacement tenant. This clearly did not happen as she was still shown as the occupant at the end of the year.

Marefield, De Vaux Place. (photo by Roy Bexon)

The attention to minor matters continued to dominate much of the discussion and following a meeting on 5 November Miss Hodding, who occupied a property that was not owned by the Dean & Chapter, was told that she could add a window on the top floor facing west as long as she obtained written agreement from her neighbour. In the 1911 census Kate Hodding was 65, and living in Chiswick with 2 servants (sisters) born in

Burcombe. She died in Salisbury in March 1934 aged 88, so it seems possible that she moved back into Close before 1917.

Following the meeting on 5 April it was agreed that the land known as Coldharbour should be transferred to the Bishop without a fee as it lay at the southern extremity of the Palace grounds. In the first three months of the year he had paid £8 3 0d in rent for Coldharbour and the site of a destroyed house in the Palace grounds.

Coldharbour. (photo by Roy Bexon)

More problematic were attempts to lease out Lower Marsh Close that had been occupied by Canon Myers. This is the northern portion of the land that exists between the two roads in the south of the Close. In the summer it hosts a cricket pitch. At the 5 February meeting the Dean & Chapter considered a letter from the secretary of the Salisbury Town Council Land Cultivation Committee who were eager to obtain Lower Marsh Close. The request was rejected claiming that the land was not suitable as it was a meadow. The 5 April meeting recorded that the field had been let to W J Snook & Co, though the 2 October meeting was told that Snook & Co had subsequently decided not to go ahead and the Clerk was authorized to rent the field to a Mr Luckham at a rent of £8 per year, but that he be allowed a rebate of £1 from the first year's rent because of the 'foul state of the field'. The rent and rebate were approved at the 5 November meeting.

Lower Marsh Close (photo by Roy Bexon)

The Dean & Chapter owned two cottages in De Vaux Place and on 3 March it was agreed to rent one of these to a soldier's wife or 'other deserving person' recommended by the Soldiers' and Sailors' Families Association at a rent of 2s 6d a week, though the tenant was not to be allowed to undertake any structural repairs and only minimal decoration was permitted as was needed to make the cottage fit for occupation. The motivation for the offer was the severe shortage of cottage accommodation in the area. Almost certainly the tenant was a Mrs Maton who lived there from early April. The other cottage in De Vaux Place was rented out at 4s 6d per week so the discount enjoyed by Mrs Maton was significant.

Clearly relations with the Town Council were not great as the minutes of the 6 February meeting recorded that the Town Clerk had asked if they could erect 'a few seats' in the Close as they would be welcomed 'by many who frequent the grounds especially in the case of old people'. The seats, they claimed, would also be beneficial to 'convalescent soldiers on warm sunny days'. Without providing any explanation, the Chapter decided to reject the application.

A further letter from the Town Clerk about an obstruction in the river was considered at the 3 August meeting and this time the Dean & Chapter were more amenable and agreed to resolve the problem.

Part of the previous year had been dominated by financial worries and the claim that Salisbury was one of the poorest cathedrals in Britain.

The medieval cathedral was endowed with land in Dorset and Wiltshire and this was added to by further endowments of land in Lincolnshire, Somerset, Berkshire, Surrey, Hampshire, Devon, Northamptonshire, Oxfordshire and Gloucestershire. The funds produced were used to finance the cathedral and to provide finance for a number of prebends that supported canons of the cathedral.

However, in 1840 the lands owned by the cathedral that lay outside the Close were transferred to the Ecclesiastical Commissioners who reallocated the total national property portfolio between all the cathedrals so as to ensure that all were adequately funded. Part of this portfolio was allocated to Salisbury, though this proved insufficient to finance the cathedral's activities and by 1916 the Dean & Chapter of Salisbury were claiming that theirs was the poorest Chapter in England. Some relief was to come in 1917 when the Ecclesiastical Commissioners agreed payments to the cathedral of £1,000 for the Dean and £500 for each Canon.

However, even with this additional help things would remain tight. Salaries for the Clerk of Works, Vergers and Close Constable amounted to £542 and payments by the Clerk of Works for general maintenance amounted to £924. In addition it is clear that the structural problems continued to provide a major

Cottages in De Vaux Place (photo by Roy Bexon)

financial challenge as on 5 June the Dean & Chapter resolved that the decayed pillars in the cloisters which were made of Tisbury stone should be replaced with Chilmark stone and treated with lime water.

Clearly the property income from houses within the Close was crucial to the financial viability of the cathedral and so dominated the considerations of the Dean & Chapter. The world may have been at war, but as this snapshot shows, for many life within the Close continued relatively unchanged. The residents were wealthy and most seemed to have servants. Some of the cathedral staff may have 'gone to war' but the liturgical life of the cathedral continued as best it could. Those who lived in the Close were largely isolated from the military activities, though throughout there was a constant fear of aircraft and the havoc they could cause. This fragile environment was dependent upon a sustainable financial structure, but with depleted resources, management of the properties within the Close became a central concern.

## Notes

1   Extract from report to the Ecclesiastical Commissioners which was discussed at the Dean & Chapter meeting of 9 May 1916.
2   Built in 1722 and known as the Oxford Chapel until 1832, now the London Institute for Contemporary Christianity.
3   See Howells J and Newman R, 2014, *Women in Salisbury Cathedral Close*, 88.

## Appendix 1
## Cathedral Receipts & Payments 1917

### Income

| | | | |
|---|---:|---:|---:|
| Rents[1] | £1,627 | 4 | 0 |
| Payment under Order in Council 1875[2] | £78 | 12 | 3 |
| Dilapidations[3] | £91 | 12 | 6 |
| Donations | £154 | 16 | 2 |
| Dividends | £1 | 19 | 4 |
| Tenants' contribution towards aircraft insurance | £153 | 14 | 11 |
| Misc sales[4] | £109 | 18 | 0 |
| | £2,217 | 17 | 2 |

### Expenditure

| | | | |
|---|---:|---:|---:|
| Income tax[5] | £393 | 0 | 5 |
| Land tax[6] | £5 | 2 | 4 |
| Rental commissions | £48 | 16 | 3 |
| Church cleaning | £70 | 0 | 0 |
| Pensions & Redeemed Land Tax | £2 | 19 | 3 |
| Queen Anne's Bounty and Tenths | £7 | 14 | 2 |

| | | | | |
|---|---|---|---|---|
| Rates on cottages in De Vaux Place | | £3 | 15 | 11 |
| Rates on Hughes House[7] | | £12 | 15 | 3 |
| Salaries[8] | | £542 | 13 | 0 |
| Vergers' Pension Scheme | | £11 | 1 | 11 |
| Insurance against fire and aircraft | | £237 | 1 | 5 |
| Clerk of Works payments | | £924 | 0 | 4 |
| Mortgage on No 64 | | £27 | 0 | 0 |
| Misc payments | | £49 | 15 | 10 |
| Loan repayment[9] | | £51 | 17 | 3 |
| | | £2,387 | 13 | 4 |

**Excess of expenditure over income** £169 16 2

Notes to Appendix 1
1 After deduction of £332 5 5 Property tax
2 Payment from Church Commissioners
3 Canon Dimont No 16 £33 2 6 , Less allowance for gates £28 10 0 , Miss Kingsbury No 7 £87 0 0
4 Sale of old materials and charges for work done for residents in the Close
5 On rentals and visitor fees
6 No 48 £1 4 1 , Verger's House £18 1 , Nos 63 & 64 £3 0 2
7 Adjoining High Street Gate
8 Clerk of Works £200; Senior Verger £125; Second Verger £85; Third Verger £37 10 0; Pupil Verger £5; Close Constable £52; Superintendent of Police £5; War Bonuses £32 10 0
9 From Prebendal Fund

## Appendix 2
## Cathedral properties in The Close

| No | Tenant | Payment | | |
|---|---|---|---|---|
| | | £ | s | d |
| 6 | W E Brigg | 35 | 0 | 0 |
| 7 | Miss Kingsbury / A A G Malet | 86 | 10 | 8 |
| 11 | EF Pye-Smith | 85 | 0 | 0 |
| 15 | Mrs Maude Coates | 105 | 0 | 0 |
| 16 | Canon Dimont / Miss H M Kingsbury | 59 | 18 | 6 |
| 19 | Trustees of Theological College | 42 | 0 | 0 |
| 20 | Canon Olivier | 102 | 0 | 0 |
| 21 | Lady Kennedy | 100 | 0 | 0 |
| 23 | Miss E H Macdonald (Rosemary Lane house) | 60 | 0 | 0 |
| 33 | W H Young (Ladywell) | 36 | 0 | 0 |
| 34 | Rev H S Anson (The Gables) | 51 | 0 | 0 |

| 35 | Hamilton Hulton (The Elms) | 60 | 0 | 0 |
| 48 | P C Bardsley | 42 | 0 | 0 |
| 50 | S Hughes (Close Constable) | | free | |
| 53 | Messrs B G & G A E Townsend (part of Mompesson House) | 53 | 0 | 0 |
| 56 | Miss L M Ottaway (Hemingsby) | 105 | 0 | 0 |
| 58 | Miss H M & M Hussey (The Wardrobe) | 100 | 0 | 0 |
| 59 | Miss A H Merrion (Arundels) | 100 | 0 | 0 |
| 63 | Training School Trustees | 50 | 0 | 0 |
| 64 | Training School Trustees | 45 | 0 | 0 |
| 68 | Mrs Jacob | 130 | 0 | 0 |
| Marefield | Mrs R E Murray | 36 | 0 | 0 |

**Cottages**

| 51 | Mrs Doris Maby | 7 | 16 | 0 |
| 66 | J Bush | 19 | 0 | 0 |
| 67 | Canon Myers/sub tenant G Allen | 14 | 6 | 0 |

**In De Vaux Place**

| | Mrs Maten | 4 | 12 | 6 |
| | Mr W J Smith | 11 | 14 | 0 |

**Various**

| Stables adjoining No 7 | Rev Dugmore | 6 | 10 | 0 |
| Toolshed in churchyard | In hand | | | |
| Rooms over High Street Gate | Mr H Messenger | 8 | 0 | 0 |
| Quit rents and redeemed land tax | | 4 | 19 | 2 |
| Pension for Lowman's House | Vicars Choral | | 15 | 6 |

**Land**

| Choristers' Green | Master of Choristers | | 6 | 8 |
| Garden in Bishop's Walk | Cecil G Bennett | 3 | 0 | 0 |
| Garden near Crane Bridge | Trustees of Church House | 2 | 10 | 0 |
| Lower Marsh Court | Rev Canon Myers/Snook & Co | 5 | 0 | 0 |
| Marsh Close | Rev A G Robertson | 7 | 0 | 0 |
| Rack Close | Training School Trustees | 20 | 0 | 0 |
| Site of girls' school in Bishop's Walk | Bishop Wordsworth trustees | 10 | 0 | 0 |
| Palace Grounds, Coldharbour & site of destroyed house | Bishop of Salisbury | 8 | 3 | 0 |
| Telephone wayleaves | | | 2 | 0 |

# The Women's Land Army in the Great War, Salisbury in 1918

## Some glimpses into the Watersmeet Hostel at Harnham

## Kate Luck

A few weeks ago I set off for Salisbury in search of Watersmeet House, a large property in Harnham, which had been used as a hostel for the Women's Land Army in the final year of the Great War. Thanks to the directions furnished by a Harnham resident who remembered seeing a sign for Watersmeet as a child, I found it very close to the Church of All Saints on Harnham Road.[1] The house, now divided into flats, is sizeable and its original garden, today the setting for several modern dwellings, must have been extensive. As I looked at the façade, I tried to imagine the comings and goings of its land girl occupants and to hear their voices, which would have been considered distinctively working-class as they were from the East End of London.

As far as I am aware, Watersmeet is not mentioned in any newspaper reports of the time, nor does it figure in the minutes of the county's War Agricultural Committee, which means that my understanding of its significance is very dependent upon a number of references to it in Edith Olivier's unpublished diaries for 1918.[2] Taken on their own, these references are somewhat sketchy but an informed reading of them suggests that Watersmeet belonged to a very challenging phase of the history of the Women's Land Army, and also that it was a particular focus of class anxiety for Olivier and the other 'lady' organizers who were overseeing the work of the WLA in Wiltshire.

*opposite page:*
Watersmeet Hostel as it appears today, photo courtesy of John Hammond

## The Women's Land Army in Wiltshire

Since 1916 Olivier had been one of the leading members of Wiltshire's Women's War Agricultural Committee (WWAC), a rather patrician group also known as 'The Ladies Committee', which was attempting to recruit women as 'emergency' land workers to fill the gap left by the male agriculturalists who had gone to the army.[3] Her diaries give a somewhat dizzying account of all that she was required to do, including overseeing teams of registrars, writing training proposals, dealing with correspondence, and compiling reports to the Board of Agriculture. In order to do this she had had to learn to drive, often with hair-raising consequences – on one occasion she came off the road and had to be towed back to Salisbury on a gun carriage – and could be seen ferrying girls to and from Salisbury railway station, or taking them to meet their new landladies and employers, or moving them between jobs when difficulties arose.

Prior to the formation of the Women's Land Army as a national body in the spring of 1917, the progress of the WWAC had been uneven. They had registered over 3,000 unskilled village women for seasonal work, had induced over 40 farmers (predominantly from South Wiltshire) to give 'on the job' instruction to small groups of students, and had opened two modest training schools. A significant problem was that that the supply of trained girls never synchronised with demands for their labour.[4] The Ladies were up against the entrenched prejudice of the majority of Wiltshire's farmers who believed that women were only capable of a narrow range of agricultural processes, that they were a relatively expensive form of labour, and that their presence on the land would allow male workers to be more readily conscripted. In practical terms, most farmers wanted women as a last resort and for the shortest time possible. Added to this, intending recruits had no wish to train during the winter in readiness for the spring, leaving the schools, as small as they were, deserted. All of this was to change in the spring of 1917 in the light of national developments.

On the 17th of October 1916, Edith Olivier recorded in her diary that she had been called to the House of Commons for a conference on agriculture, where the Director General for Recruiting had come from the War Office to say 'quite privately' that the army needed 100,000 more men for the coming Spring offensive and that they would be taken 'whether a substitute is to be had or not'. She continued 'they seem to expect our Women's Comtee [sic] to fill the gap'. Directly afterwards, she went to tea with her cousin Sydney Olivier who was Permanent Secretary to the Board of Agriculture, in order to discuss 'various plans of working Wiltshire to grapple with the new problem'.[5]

By November food stocks were so low that the President of the Board of Agriculture estimated that the nation was just weeks away from starvation.[6] This crisis led the government to launch a number of 'interventionist' reforms designed to control, regularise, and modernise agriculture, amongst which was the creation of the Women's Land Army as a national, civilian, uniformed force, working under the direction of the Board's Food Production Department. The Ladies Committee was now expected to work with the WLA under National Service regulations with the guidance of a 'lady' inspector from the

WLA armbands were awarded after three months service. The owner of this armband received a red diamond for two years' service and a 'Good Service' patch for her exemplary performance. Photo from author's collection.

Women's Section of the Food Production Department, and alongside a paid County Organizer and Labour Exchanges. They were also launching a new training scheme on behalf of Wiltshire's Agricultural Education Committee which only considered applicants born within the county, these two schemes running side by side.[7]

At its inception the Women's Land Army was aiming to recruit 'educated', patriotic, town-bred young women who, it was assumed, would have a bracing effect on declining rural communities. As she waited for the first of these WLA 'lasses' to arrive, Olivier's diary entries suggest a level of anxiety about making preparations for them, particularly around issues of class. During February 1917 she had been busy moving existing students between two new training schools, segregating a working class element at Manningford (in the Vale of Pewsey) and taking the 'educated' [upper class] ones to Longford Castle which would also house the newly arrived WLA girls.[8] Olivier, who shared the class assumptions of her charmed social circle, was therefore dismayed to find that at least some of the new arrivals for Longford fell well below the expected standard, describing two of those she was collecting from the railway station as '*awful*, not "educated" at all, but real dirty slum girls or so *we* thought. They both nearly had hysterics on the platform'.[9]

These class preconceptions were to be much tested in the final year of the war as the Women's Land Army, very short of recruits, actively sought to enrol working-class girls from London, particularly from Woolwich and the East End, staging huge recruitment rallies and relaxing their admissions criteria. As an inducement, it became possible to sign up for only six months, and unfit girls were given a period of probationary light training in the hope that country life would nurse them back to health.[10] The Food Production Department was concerned that these working-class recruits would prove totally unsuited to agricultural work and to rural surroundings. Deputy Director Edith Lyttelton characterised them as temperamental and volatile, and unable to overcome difficulties or rationally express their grievances without a great deal of support.[11] There ensued an exchange of correspondence between the Food Production Department and the county WWACs which focused on issues of discipline and welfare, on one hand stressing the need to keep the new girls in check so that they did not dishonour their uniform and displease the farmers who employed them, and on the other hand underlining the need to befriend them and keep them happy.[12]

## The London girls come to Salisbury

At the end of April the *Wiltshire Gazette*, a strong supporter of the 'Women on the Land Movement', provided a glowing description of one of the London rallies. This emphasized its friendly and picturesque aspect. The Land Army girls present were described as having 'all the regalia of the farmyard about them', with some girls carrying hens, rabbits, pigs and lambs while 'a pretty shepherdess tramped along with her sheep dog at her heels'. Others had carried axes and four-legged stools to represent forestry and dairy.

The paper gave an equally disarming account of the new London recruits, emphasising their patriotism and pointing out that 'they could get much better money at munitions'. It was claimed that many of them had not worked before the war, possibly with the inference that they had not been contaminated by the harshness and vulgarity which was often presumed to be the legacy of factory work, possibly to suggest that they were from comfortably off backgrounds. The Gazette was sure that, in any case, country life would change them, for the 'frail little town

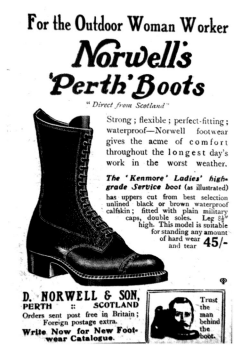

For the Outdoor Woman Worker

**Norwell's 'Perth' Boots**

" *Direct from Scotland* "

Strong ; flexible ; perfect-fitting ; waterproof—Norwell footwear gives the acme of comfort throughout the longest day's work in the worst weather.

*The 'Kenmore' Ladies' high-grade Service boot* (as illustrated) has uppers cut from best selection unlined black or brown waterproof calfskin ; fitted with plain military caps, double soles. Leg 8¼" high. This model is suitable for standing any amount of hard wear and tear **45/-**

**D. NORWELL & SON,**
PERTH :: SCOTLAND
Orders sent post free in Britain ; Foreign postage extra.
**Write Now for New Foot-wear Catalogue.**

Trust the man behind the boot.

An advert for stout work boots aimed at women land workers, *Women at Home* magazine, January 1918

girls' who had previously arrived in Wiltshire were, by dint of fresh work and hard toil, so changed that their own parents would not recognise them.[13]

According to Olivier's memoir, the London recruits were dispatched to the counties which needed them in groups of 20 or 30. Those destined for Wiltshire were tested for a fortnight or so before they were finally accepted and each one was interviewed by Olivier in person on the day of arrival. She remembered the 'ignorance' of these new arrivals, claiming that they 'were quite unsuitable for farm work. Two of the would-be milkers were terrified at their first sight of a cow, having expected they would look like joints of beef hanging in butchers' shops which had hitherto been their only acquaintance with cattle'.[14]

The recruitment of girls under the National Service scheme had created a demand for extra accommodation and Edith Olivier started to look into the possibility of opening a large hostel. She and Lady Pembroke first visited Watersmeet House in May, climbing in through a window when they found that the land agent had lost the keys. The house was big enough for their purposes but in dire need of cleaning as it had recently been vacated by 80 American soldiers. Olivier and Lady Pembroke estimated that it could accommodate 40 girls.[15] Soon after they agreed a rent of 30 shillings per week and set about finding farmers willing to train the girls.[16] By the end of June 1917 it was ready for the first arrivals, although so sparsely furnished that Olivier described it as 'Horrible, so bare. Not a single comfort, just beds in the rooms & naught else'. Arrangements were made to organize food rations for the hostel as a system of rationing was being rolled out nationally at this time, and Olivier had had to visit the police station and shops to facilitate this just before the girls' arrival. When the first girls, expected on the 27th did not arrive, Olivier phoned Miss Tennant, the Board of Agriculture's paid organiser, who told her none were coming. Olivier commented 'luckily we had not yet cooked the meat'.[17] The first intake came on the 1st of July, which Olivier described as 'A busy day. Three times to Watersmeet & to station & round the town getting provisions in my car, Mrs Lavington in & out & much driving. Ten girls came at 3 oc [o'clock] from London. They look not bad & I made an oration asking them to keep up the honour of the Hostel. Mrs Lavington has too low an idea of their character & Miss Clapham too high! I hope the new Matron will be the golden mean'.[18] In actual fact the new matron, Mrs Albino, was judged to be 'a large blue lazy slug – a dreadful beast' and had to be dismissed. It was decided that Mrs Lavington, who had been living in a caravan so as to be fully mobile, should take her place as she was getting too old to continue as a gang leader.[19]

Olivier, who had obviously taken on board the advice of the FPD, proceeded to oversee Watersmeet using an approach which combined friendliness with the need for surveillance. In the first days after their arrival, she kept a close eye on the new intake, arranged entertainments for them, and made sure that they understood their responsibilities as representatives of the WLA.

Olivier and Lady Pembroke had planned a large scale event which would introduce the new recruits to existing land workers, and smooth their way with the local community. This was a 'Land Girls Party' for 450 guests which took place in the garden of Wilton House on the occasion of the Silver Wedding of the King and Queen.[20] A lively affair, this featured an Australian band and 'Pierrots', who were a great success. The girls, who were 'all so happy and natural & looking vy [very] nice in their uniforms' were delighted to receive an answer to the telegram they had sent to the royal couple.[21]

On the following day, the Watersmeet girls were honoured by a visit from Sir Henry Sclator, a distinguished and much decorated soldier, at this time serving as General Officer-in-Chief for Southern Command and resident at Cliff House in Harnham. Olivier noted that he had raised a Union Flag and made a faltering speech to the girls, presumably a patriotic pep-talk. Olivier commented that this was 'quite a nice hello ceremony & it sets the key for the Hostel'.[22]   A few days later, Lady Pembroke and Gwen Plunkett Greene (daughter of Sir Hubert Parry, composer of *Jerusalem*) paid another visit of a formal nature, with the girls lining up outside the property to receive them in an 'imposing' manner prior to an inspection of the whole hostel.[23]

On the second evening after their arrival, Olivier had motored over to the hostel to teach the girls 'a Greek dance' with a view to them performing it later in the month.[24] This was clearly in line with the WLA directive to provide Land Army girls with recreational activities, under the assumption these were of particular importance for girls who had come from cities and were thus used to livelier surroundings. It was also an ideal way to introduce the girls to their neighbours. At their dress rehearsal, at the Hollies at Ford, the girls 'looked delicious in the Greek dresses against a big hedge, all pink roses'.[25] Two days later they danced again at a social evening at the hostel, at which Olivier and Judith Alcock sang, and Marion Alcock played the cello. At the end of the evening the girls danced to a gramophone, provided by Edith's sister, Mildred, and socialised 'with a few lame soldiers with whom they walked arm in arm'.[26]

Olivier also made sure that the girls had reading matter. They could buy *The Landswoman* which was the official magazine of the WLA and the WI, launched the previous January as 'a paper friend'. There was also a magazine written specifically for Wiltshire's women land workers called *The Turnip* which had first appeared in November 1917 with a handsome green and gold cover and was the brainchild of Olivier and Celia Furse, daughter of Sir Henry Newbolt of Netherhampton House. Furse was also assembling a lending library for them.[27]

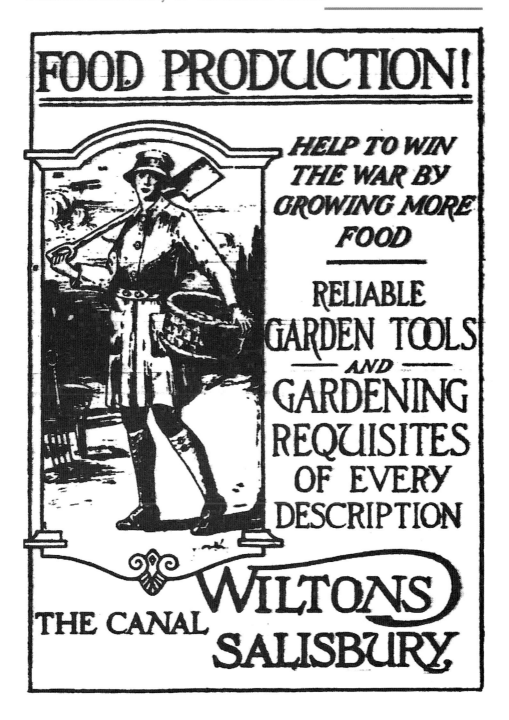

A depiction of a land girl in her distinctive uniform with breeches, from *The Salisbury Journal* 16 March 1918

It was not all plain sailing, and there were some initial teething problems with the hostel. Often the information supplied by the Board's paid organiser proved to be unreliable and Olivier spent much time at the railway station needlessly awaiting arrivals, or fetching back girls who had been dispatched to the wrong placements.[28] There was also some difficulty with arranging training. Olivier had to meet with the irate wives of dairymen who were refusing to allow their husbands to teach the girls how to milk. She commented 'We were threatened with brickbats but got home. It felt like canvassing at an Election'. Although the 'angriest' of these women later relented and declared herself not 'a bit jealous', that such opposition had been expressed in the first place suggests a prejudice against these 'outsiders', possibly because they were considered to be more alluring or morally lax, or both, than country girls.[29]

Questions of decency and decorum were of fundamental interest to the Women's Land Army and members were exhorted to uphold 'the dignity of the uniform' by abstaining from smoking, swearing, and drinking in public houses. The influx of soldiers into Salisbury had led to an increase in disorderly behaviour and fears had been voiced that they posed a moral threat to young women.[30] They would have been perceived as an obvious temptation to the young women of the Land Army who were away from home, making it necessary to 'police' their conduct in mixed company by arranging events where their contact with the opposite sex could be controlled. Instances of girls exhibiting 'flighty' behaviour or becoming entangled in unsuitable relationships did arise – however, there is not enough evidence to ascertain whether the girls involved were more likely to come from London or other large cities. Olivier records only one such instance, and that not very serious, in relation to Watersmeet in August 1918 when she 'stopped at Harnham to jaw the girls for hanging about the gate with soldiers'.[31]

We know that for one girl from the hostel this fraternization had a happy outcome. This was Tilly (Matilda) Alden who married a private in the American army on the 14th (and the 16th!) of September 1918. The bride came from a solidly working class East End background.[32] According to her wedding certificate she was 19 at the time of her marriage and gave her occupation as 'L.A.A.S.', in other words the Land Army Agricultural Section. The groom, James Ellison, 23, gave his occupation as 'Aviation Section, U.S.A', and his place of residence as Lopcombe Corner, Grately. Described in Olivier's diary as a 'flying man', the groom was actually part of an airfield construction crew supporting the U S aero squadrons of the American Expeditionary Force. He could not have been in England long since he had not been drafted until December 1917[33]

Things did not go exactly as planned. Although Geoffrey Hill, the vicar of All Saints, attested on the wedding certificate that the couple were married

iage solemnized at *the Register Office*
n the **District** of *Salisbury* in the **County** of

| Name and Surname. | Age. | Condition. | Rank or Profession. | Residence at the time of Marriage. |
|---|---|---|---|---|
| James Henry Ellison | 23 years | Bachelor | No 1335788 Private Aviation Section American Army | 2nd Construction Coy. B.C. Aviation Section Boscombe Down Hants |
| Matilda Alden | 19 years | Spinster | Land Worker L.A.A.S. | Watersmeet Hostel East Harnham Salisbury |

*Register Office* according to the Rites and Ceremonies of the
*...us Henry Ellison.* in the *Mich'ale Henry Alder*
*...tilda Alden* Presence of us, *...auth nane Olivier*

Detail of Tilly Alden's first marriage certificate, September 1918

'according to the rites and ceremonies of the established church', he later added a note to the effect that the certificate was an 'irregular entry as no ecclesiastical preliminaries [possibly the reading of banns] had been gone through... 'and they had therefore had to have a second ceremony two days later in Salisbury Registry Office.[34] Edith Olivier described the second service as a most depressing affair – 'a dreadful ceremony, a dirty office, solicitors' clerks writing, solicitors making polite & otiose remarks – an interminable interview but so unimpressive that she might well forget she was married & think she had only been to see the lawyer about a fire insurance policy which would run out if not renewed!'[35]

Unfortunately, as the war was drawing to its end it becomes more difficult [for us] to follow the story of Watersmeet as changes in Olivier's role alter the focus of her diary. Towards the end of July the Board of Agriculture appointed her paid Organizing Secretary for the entire county. Her replacement, Lady Kathleen Thynne, the daughter of the Marquis of Bath, was not available until late September but from this point took on the day to day running of the hostel and the minor difficulties which arose, liaising with Olivier only when disciplinary measures, such as Courts Martial, were called for.[36]

Accordingly, the final glimpse we have of Watersmeet concerns a girl whom Edith Olivier was called to discipline on charges of drunkenness on the 18th November 1918. This was 'the morning after' the day of the great Peace Thanksgiving Service which had been celebrated in Salisbury Cathedral. Olivier writes that she was called 'to see & presumably discharge a woman who got drunk yesterday but her story touched me so that I have given her another chance'.[37]

Olivier's memoir identifies the culprit as Mrs Harding who was the London born wife of a serving Canadian soldier and had only been in Wiltshire for a few days. Looking desperately ill and not strong enough for farm work when she had first arrived, Harding had excused her pallor by saying that she had been unable to find the cosmetics she required in Salisbury which was 'rather a one-horse place'. It was only after the Thanksgiving Service, a few days later that the true nature of her problem emerged when the matron of the hostel reported that she had been roaring drunk the night before. She had been sick all over her bedroom, and was now in 'a most wilful and defiant mood'. On being called, Olivier expected that she would have to deal with 'a virago' but found her miserable and unwell. Harding then explained that she was the daughter of drunkards and had been rescued from them by a philanthropic society which sent her to Canada. She had never tasted drink until she returned to London to live with her sister, also a drunkard, and feared that she would be dead within the month if sent back. At this point Olivier asked her to sign a pledge of abstinence and told her that she would be discharged if she broke it. However, Olivier was concerned that she would not remain sober if sent to work on a farm because she would be alone amongst strangers.[38]

Fortunately, from early 1918 organizers had the option of diverting women not suited to agricultural work into forage or forestry. Olivier seems to have moved girls between sections as demand dictated and at this time had some of the Watersmeet girls cutting timber in Grovely Wood. Her solution to Harding's problem was to send her there even though she was a skilled milker and conditions in the forest were primitive. The positives were that she would be with a gang she knew and presumably alcohol would be in shorter supply. Olivier wrote 'I have never felt more sorry for anyone, and I greatly admired the way in which the other women rallied round her and helped her along'.[39]

In Grovely the Watersmeet girls were working alongside women whom Olivier described as 'unregistered' with the inference that they had fallen below the standard required for the WLA, including one girl who had been discharged after an affair with a married farmer. Grovely would have been an ideal place to 'contain' such girls as it was relatively remote and they would have been working directly for the county rather than employed by a farmer. In another instance, she found farm work for an art student from London who claimed she had been mixed up with a jewel thief and could not supply a reference.[40] Although Olivier thought this so much 'cock and bull', the fact that she was finding work for women whom she would not have considered even one year earlier is an indication of just how much her attitudes had needed to change.

After the demobilisation of the Women's Land Army in November 1919, Edith Lyttelton expressed the hope that many of the 'poorer class of town girl' would remain on the land rather than return to the ruinous conditions of city life which would make them 'shiftless and irresponsible'.[41]  In contrast, The *Wiltshire Gazette* opined that these girls had been fundamentally changed by their experience of land work, for 'the loafer and the unintelligent factory girl have left apathy behind, and mere wage earners have developed into enthusiasts. Patriotic instincts for the most part unknown to this class of girl, gave keenness at the start and *esprit de corps* as time went on ... new effort literally kindled her into life'.[42]  Clearly both of these views were shaped by a mythology of class and a concept of natural renewal which had survived the war. Unfortunately, apart from Tilly Ellison who emigrated in March 1919 and became a naturalised American, and Mrs Harding who returned to married life in Canada, the post-war fortunes of the *Watersmeet* girls cannot be known.

## Notes

1   I am indebted to Kathy Quinn, President of the Salisbury Local History Group, who identified the location of the house for me. Also to William Alexander (Archivist for Harnham Parish) who has furnished me with information relating to the history of the house, which was built on the site of Watersmeet Farm in 1869 for Henry Rogers, a Whiting manufacturer, on land belonging to Lord Radnor. It stood next to the Whiting factory and was known as Prospect House until at least 1904.

2   Olivier, Edith, unpublished diaries, Wiltshire and Swindon Archives 982/49 and 982/50

3   *War Agricultural Committee Minutes*, 14 January 1916 WSA F1/100/23

4   *War Agricultural Committee Minutes* 14 July 1916 WSA F1/100/23. 'Women Farm Workers; Over 2,000 Employed in Wilts' 22 July 1916, *Wiltshire Times*

5   Olivier, Edith, diary, 17 October 1916, WSA 982/50

6   Lord Ernle (Prothero, Roland), 1925, Chapter V1 "The Food Campaign 1916-1918" in *The Land and Its People*, Cambridge University Press

7   'County Council's Training Scheme' 25 Jan 1917,*Wiltshire Gazette*

8   Olivier, Edith, diary, 6 and 10 February 1918, WSA 982/48,

9   Olivier, Edith, diary, 28 February 1918, WSA 982/48,

10  Scott, Caroline, 2017, *Holding the Home Front; The Women's Land Army in the First World War* , Pen and Sword History, 104,113

11  Lyttelton, The Hon Mrs Alfred, October 1918, 'The Women's Land Army' *Journal of the Board of Agriculture,* 809

12  White, Bonnie, 2014,*The Women's Land Army in First World War Britain* Palgrave Macmillan, 94-95

13  'Land Girls March in London', 25 April 1918,*Wiltshire Gazette*

14  Olivier, Edith 1939, *Without Knowing Mr Walkley; Personal Memories*, Faber and Faber, 217-218

15  Olivier, Edith, diary 25 May 1918 ,WSA  982/49

16  Olivier, Edith diary,  4 and 13 June 1918,WSA 982/49

17  Olivier, Edith, diary, 25 to 27 June 1918, WSA 982/49,

18  Olivier, Edith, diary,  1 July 1918, WSA 982/49

19  Olivier, Edith, diary,  10 July 1918, WSA 982/49

20  George V and Queen Mary of Teck

21  Olivier, Edith, diary,  6 July 1918 ,WSA 982/49

22  Olivier, Edith, diary, 7 July 1918 ,WSA 982/49,

23  Olivier, Edith, diary,  11 July 1918, WSA 982/49

24  Olivier, Edith, diary, 2 July 1918, WSA 982/49

25  Olivier, Edith diary, 13 July 1918, WSA 982/49,

26  Olivier, Edith, diary, 15 July 1918, WSA 982/49,

27  Olivier, Edith, diary, 11 July 1918, WSA 982/49

28  Olivier, Edith, diary, 8 July 1918, WSA 982/49

29  Olivier, Edith, diary, 16 July 1918, WSA 982/49,

30  Olivier, Edith, diary, 18 and 22 January 1915, WSA 982/47

31  Olivier, Edith, diary, 10 August 1918, WSA 982/49

32  The 1911 census shows her living on the Old Kent Road with her parents, several siblings, and an elderly lodger. Her father's occupation is given as a 'Flour Carman', while her older sisters worked as a tin box maker and an errand girl.

33  U S Passport Application 1795-1925, wives of members of the AEF in Europe, Vol. 003

34  Register of Marriages 1854-1959 WSA 1045/3

35  Olivier, Edith, diary, 16 September 1918, WSA 982/50

36  Olivier, Edith, diary, 20 September 1918, WSA 982/50

37  Olivier, Edith, diary, 18 November 1918, WSA 982/50

38  Olivier, Edith, 1939, *Without Knowing Mr Walkley,* Faber and Faber, 218-221

39  Olivier, Edith, 1939, *Without Knowing Mr Walkley,* Faber and Faber,221

40  Olivier , Edith,1939, *Without Knowing Mr Walkley* ,Faber and Faber, 222

41  Lyttelton, The Hon Mrs Alfred, October 1918 'The Women's Land Army, *Journal of the Board of Agriculture,* 809

42  'Women's Land Army: A Retrospect' 25 March 1920,*Wiltshire Gazette*

# Kingston Deverill
# A South West Wiltshire Village

## by Julian Wiltshire

The Hobnob Press ISBN 978-1-906978-41-9 263 pp £12.95
[Available from the author via julianwiltshire@btinternet.com and from
Waterstones.)

In this account of the village in which he lives, Julian Wiltshire has balanced attention to detail with the bigger and changing picture over many centuries. It is therefore both a reference book collating historical and social facts as well as a compelling story of human interest.

In moving to Kingston Deverill, the author recalled his time as an undergraduate translating the *Anglo-Saxon Chronicle* and encountering that moment in 878 AD when King Alfred passed through where Dorset, Somerset and Wiltshire now meet, on his way to defeat the Danish army. A stopping point en route is mentioned as 'Ecgbryhtesstan' or Egbert's Stones, traditionally believed to be a venue for council meetings led by Egbert, Alfred's grandfather. These sarsen stones, albeit without their original lintel, are still to be found in Kingston Deverill as a testament to those times.

From being a geographical place of political significance, the history of this village in the Deverill Valley is one of responses to local and national influences. The presence of different landed families are shown, with the Thynnes seated at Longleat emerging as patrons in the eighteenth century. Their involvement with the village is charted in the first two chapters, particularly in terms of church and clergy. A site of worship since the eleventh century, records no longer exist that record the origins of the medieval construction of the church, although the date of the earliest registered rector is 1302. Since then Christian witness and worship have continued there via the Victorian restoration to the present day.

The development of Kingston Deverill School from its foundation by the Marchioness of Bath in 1840 is the subject of chapter three. There are judicious entries from the later ongoing school logbook and the author's comments provide insights into changing patterns of life as well as education:

*Kingston Deverill*

A SOUTH WEST WILTSHIRE VILLAGE

*Julian Wiltshire*

> *1902 –June 11: During the hay-making season school commenced at 1.30, dismissed at 3.45.* This is an interesting indication of the continuing dependence on the help of young children in the fields in the early Edwardian era......
> *1938 – June 1: the children told to look both ways when crossing road.* Traffic now increasing in both directions – namely from both Mere and Warminster.

Records of the development of agriculture are provided in the fourth chapter written by Richard and David Stratton, two generations of a farming family. They also look at the bigger changes over time caused by external forces and the need for farmers to adjust purposes, methods and technology to survive with 'our thin, hungry and leached soils'.

The declining agricultural workforce is one of many developments that can be traced in the final and longest chapter *The Social Scene* in which Julian Wiltshire draws upon entries in the National Censuses from 1841 to 1911. The impact in the twentieth century of the wider world of wars, economic vagaries and new technology is inevitably a part of the record of constant change. What, however, is heartening is the evidence of the heart of village life beating strongly, of a community that has grown more inclusive in recent years and which continues to celebrate the blessings of its setting.

The author is a Wiltshireman if not by birth then most certainly by surname and long residency in the county. He has written a scholarly history that is thoughtful, sympathetic and with pleasing touches of humour. The book has several useful appendices, is well illustrated, and its cover and frontispiece feature most attractive watercolours by Chris Littlemore.

John Cox

## Author Biographies 2017

**Ruth Butler** was a teacher and former journalist. She is currently Heritage Education Officer at the Wiltshire and Swindon History Centre, using the archives to develop and deliver heritage and cultural learning across the county. She was previously education officer at The Salisbury Museum. Since 2013 Ruth has focused her research on the First World War and is part of the Wiltshire at War project team which is currently working on the last of five community exhibitions.

**John Chandler** is currently consultant editor for the Victoria County History in Gloucestershire and Wiltshire, and has researched and published extensively on the history of places in Wiltshire and Dorset, especially the Salisbury area. He was formerly general editor of the Wiltshire Record Society and joint editor of *Wiltshire Studies.*

**John Cox** has lived in Salisbury since 1979 when he became Head of English at Bishop Wordsworth's School and where he directed over thirty dramatic productions before retiring as Assistant Headteacher in 2010. He attends St. Thomas's Church and is a trustee of three local charities: *EdUKaid, La Folia,* and *Sarum St. Michael Educational Charity.* He joined the editorial board of *Sarum Chronicle* in 2014.

**John Elliott** is an architectural historian who used to teach at the University of Reading and the University of London, Royal Holloway and Bedford New College. He is now retired and lives near Salisbury.

**Sharon Evans** is a retired doctor and resident of Laverstock with links, past and present, to St Andrew's school. As no one else in the Laverstock Local History Group had taken up the suggestion of researching the school's history, she embarked on historical research for the first time, and found it fascinating.

**Anthony Hamber**, a native of Salisbury, is an independent photographic historian. He has previously published a biography of William Blackmore,

*Collecting the American West: The Rise and Fall of William Blackmore,* Hobnob Press, 2010. He is currently completing a major study of the impact of photography at the 1851 Great Exhibition.

**Peter Hoare** FSA was University Librarian at the University of Nottingham for fifteen years; since moving to Salisbury in retirement he has worked in the Cathedral Library as a volunteer. Among a lifetime's research in the field of library history, he was general editor of the *Cambridge History of Libraries in Britain and Ireland* (3 vols, 2006).

**Jane Howells** is editor of *Local History News* for the British Association for Local History. She wrote a new introduction to the 2013 reprint of Maud Davies's *Life in an English Village* (Hobnob Press). With Ruth Newman she transcribed and edited William Small's *Cherished Memories and Associations* (Wiltshire Record Society 2011), and they are the authors of *Women in Salisbury Cathedral Close,* Sarum Studies 5, 2014.

**Kate Luck** is a retired lecturer (including at the renowned Bath Academy of Art) with a background in Art and Design History, and a doctorate in Costume History. She is currently researching the part played by women in agriculture in Wiltshire, with emphasis on the Women's Land Army, in both world wars. She is also a 1940s re-enactor.

**Andrew Minting** is a conservation officer with Wiltshire Council based in Salisbury. He is also currently involved with projects for the Institute of Historic Building Conservation and Historic England that aim to improve the content and accessibility of historic built environment information through the Heritage Gateway website and local Historic Environment Records.

**Joe Newman** has had an interest in railways, and steam locomotives in particular, for over 70 years. He taught chemistry at Bishop Wordsworth's School for 36 years and was Deputy Headmaster there from 1976 to 1998. He is currently the coffee maker to the *Sarum Chronicle* editorial board.

**Ruth Newman** is the co-author with Jane Howells of *Salisbury Past,* and in 2011 they edited and transcribed William Small's *Cherished Memories and Associations* for the Wiltshire Record Society. They have more recently written *Women in Salisbury Cathedral Close,* Sarum Studies 5, 2014. She is both a Blue Badge and Cathedral guide.

**Louise Purdy** has been a volunteer with the charity the Wiltshire Buildings Record since 2005, which is based at the Wiltshire and Swindon History Centre. She is a researcher within one of their teams which investigates historic buildings and charts their evolution. In 2010 she obtained an Undergraduate Advanced Diploma in Local History from the University of Oxford.

**Philip Rabbetts** worked in the petrochemical industry and some 40 years ago started to study his family history. He quickly discovered that his male line came from south Wiltshire. He is now chairman and programme secretary of the Salisbury branch of Wiltshire Family History Society.

**David Richards** is a retired dental surgeon who is now a Blue Badge Guide with a particular interest in the history of the people and buildings of the Salisbury area.

**Tim Tatton-Brown** is a freelance archaeologist and architectural historian, with a particular interest in ecclesiastical buildings. He is consultant archaeologist to St George's Chapel, Windsor, and to Westminster School and Lambeth Palace.

**Anne Trevett** is a founder trustee of the Bemerton Community charity and one of the team of fund raisers who worked on the project. She is chair of Bemerton Local History Society

**Stuart Wakefield** developed his interest in history only after retiring in 2010, when he went to live in Kuala Lumpur where he provided tours in the National Museum. After returning to the UK, he completed a Masters in Local History with the Open University, and now plans to undertake a PhD.

**Peter Webster** became a self-employed information management consultant on leaving the Army in 1992 after a full career in the Royal Corps of Signals. Now retired, he remains an active member of the local community in Lower Bemerton, and was Chairman of Bemerton Community Ltd. from its foundation in 2009 until 2014.